THE
FUTURE
ECONOMY
AND INCLUSIVE
COMPETITIVENESS®

HOW DEMOGRAPHIC **TRENDS** AND **INNOVATION** CAN CREATE ECONOMIC **PROSPERITY** FOR **ALL** AMERICANS

JONATHAN M. HOLIFIELD, J.D.

FOREWORD BY JAY WILLIAMS, FORMER U.S. ASSISTANT
SECRETARY OF COMMERCE FOR ECONOMIC DEVELOPMENT

The Future Economy and Inclusive Competitiveness®
How Demographic Trends and Innovation Can Create Economic Prosperity for All Americans

Johnathan M. Holifield, J.D.

Published by: ScaleUp Partners LLC
www.ScaleUpPartners.com

ISBN: 978-0692877708

PRAISE FOR THE FUTURE ECONOMY AND INCLUSIVE COMPETITIVENESS®

"Brilliant! Unlike any other book written on economic development, this one encapsulates the challenges and opportunities of the nation through the lens of economic inclusion and competitiveness ideals. Johnathan has provided America a treasured asset that will continue to grow dividends over time and offer a wealth of knowledge to benefit generations to come."

Jay Williams
Former U.S. Assistant Secretary of Commerce for Economic Development
Administrator, Economic Development Administration

"As the former Lt. Governor of Ohio whose responsibility it was to direct Ohio's economic development strategy, I believe that Holifield's ideas on how to improve U.S. global economic performance while tapping into our country's talented and diverse innovators, entrepreneurs, and workforce are on point. It's a timely and important contribution to the emerging national discourse."

Lee Fisher
Interim Dean and Visiting Professor of Law, Cleveland-Marshall College of Law, Cleveland State University
Senior Advisor, CEOs for Cities

"Holifield has provided important and vital lessons about what really drives and sustains national economic success. This well-documented treatise filled with pride and passion points America to a future where intentionality towards inclusivity—realizing the potential of all our people—ensures our economic longevity."

Clifton L. Taulbert
Entrepreneur, Pulitzer-Nominated Author & International Lecturer
Author of *Once Upon A Time When We Were Colored*

"Holifield has delivered a critical work for policymakers, decision-makers, and community leaders who care about the health of our nation's economy. As Holifield suggests, by investing in economic inclusion and competitiveness, we can unleash a new wave of economic development and strengthen our long-term global advantage. Ignoring the important lessons and practical tools laid out in this book would be at our peril."

Christopher Gergen
CEO, Forward Impact

"The Future Economy and Inclusive Competitiveness explains what an inclusive prosperity built on one economy for all Americans will mean—and warns what we risk losing if we don't. Read it to cut through the noise—the political posturing, the economic smoke and mirrors, and the media haze. It is a balanced, pointed, and timely call to action. Holifield makes clear what we need to do."

Mark Pinsky
Author of *Opportunity for All*
Former CEO, Opportunity Finance Network

"With a fresh voice, Holifield clearly identifies the economic imperative of our time. Prescribing a realignment of underserved community priorities to incorporate economic competitiveness, his restructuring framework is perceptive, coherent, and transcends political affiliations. It will appeal to Republicans, Democrats, and independents alike. This book is an enlightening and empowering read for civil and human rights activists and leaders."

Michael Schreiber
Chief Operating Officer, Robert F. Kennedy Human Rights

"Since meeting Johnathan in 2013 during my Travelling Fellowship to the U.S., I have followed his innovative work with a strong interest in how his ideas can be transferred to the United Kingdom. With his new book, we now have a blueprint to not only build a vibrant and diverse economy but to also work towards eliminating social and economic inequalities both here in the U.K. as well as the U.S."

Roger Warnock
Clore Social Fellow (2016)
Fellow, Winston Churchill Memorial Trust

"Johnathan Holifield rightfully points out that if our country is to maintain its position of economic leadership in the world, we must unearth the hidden gifts of all Americans—including, Blacks, Latinos, women, and rural populations. Moreover, he lays forward a clearly defined and exciting path for accomplishing this. Every mayor and government leader in the United States should read this book."

Mayor Byron W. Brown
City of Buffalo

"Johnathan's Inclusive Competitiveness® framework is vital for education leaders, especially at our treasured historically Black colleges and universities. His defined vision to keep the U.S. a global economic powerhouse by providing a good education that empowers our deep well of diverse talent is essential for the common good. This book should be consumed and made actionable by educators, policymakers, philanthropists, and corporate leaders alike."

Dr. Leonard L. Haynes, III
Senior Director, Institutional Services, U.S. Dept. of Education (Ret.)
Former Executive Director, White House Initiative on Historically Black
Colleges and Universities

"Holifield presents a powerful vision for how the United States can sustain economic growth and wealth creation well in to the future. His vision is based on a compelling modern view of the wealth of nations which is bound up in the interconnectedness of innovation, implementable ideas, and networks of the various ethnic and racial groups. Simply put, Holifield argues that the size and robustness of the future U.S. economy is a matter of recognizing the 'demographic shift' of our country and implementing best practices to include the value and talent from all ethnic groups."

Dr. Ronald A. Johnson
President, Clark Atlanta University

"The pioneering framework in this book has the potential to increase access to and improve performance of our nation's Innovation Economy, which translates to more startup and high-growth companies, better nonproft and public organizations, more jobs, and more education across the board. Together, we have the power to make America the global model of twenty-first century education and economic inclusion and competitiveness."

Dr. Roderick J. McDavis
President, Ohio University

FOREWORD

Since the end of armed conflict on the battlefields of World War II, the U.S. has dominated and achieved momentous victories on the battlefields of global economics. Interestingly, we did this with one hand proverbially tied behind our back, as so much of our population has been underutilized, neglected, and overlooked in the process.

Today, America is at a critical tipping point in our history: the demography of the country is changing rapidly, with women comprising more than half our population, the number of Blacks growing steadily, and dramatic increases in the numbers of Hispanics. By and large, these populations still struggle to access leading education and economic opportunities. Moreover, we are also experiencing the consequences of the proximity of opportunity, where far too many small town and rural White populations are geographically separated from our nation's most promising career and entrepreneurship pathways.

To maintain our leading competitive position in the world and successfully compete in this century, America must make sure *everyone* is on the playing field–that we're tapping into the ingenuity and creativity of all segments of society and spreading our best opportunities to every corner of the country. President Obama has often said that the talent necessary to keep America as the most innovative and dynamic economy on the planet is spread across every corner of the country; however, the opportunity to participate is not.

Most significantly, however, if we continue down the road of concentrating our top education and economic opportunities among a small number of Americans at the expense of broad, inclusive, and enduring prosperity, we risk irreversibly damaging our democracy and surrendering the very egalitarian and meritocratic ideals that make America exceptional in the world.

In my position as U.S. assistant secretary of commerce for economic development and administrator of the EDA, I was tapped by President Obama to lead the federal economic development agenda by promoting innovation and competitiveness, thereby preparing American regions for growth and success worldwide. My highest priority has been working to achieve those ends by improving the competitiveness and elevating the living standards of all Americans.

Born, raised, and educated in Youngstown, Ohio, and having experienced the economic transition of the nation away from manufacturing to a knowledge-based, tech-driven Innovation Economy, I have seen the devastation suffered in the "Rust Belt" firsthand, as well as the struggles of families and communities addressing severe economic challenges in the Midwest. I've also spent considerable time on the ground in "coal county" and other parts of rural America and have been struck by the similarities of the experiences of feeling left behind and disconnected.

It is that personal and professional experience at all levels of the socioeconomic spectrum that generates a genuine excitement about the way forward articulated by Johnathan Holifield in this book. With discerning clarity, he explains the economic conditions of this nation and how a demographically and geographically diverse landscape of innovative Americans can compete and win the future in a global economy without regard to who occupies the Oval Office.

Johnathan also understands the devastating impact that the twenty-first century evolution to an Innovation Economy has had on communities and regions that relied upon the manufacturing sector for employment and other economic opportunities. In the midst of this mess, he sees opportunities and begins to delineate a clear pathway for those most affected. Even the most studied economist and seasoned civic, government, and philanthropic leader will find enlightening information in every chapter of this book.

The Future Economy and Inclusive Competitiveness® should be included in the studies at every high school, college, and university in the nation. Research institutions, foundations, and government leaders should invest time in poring over the extraordinary amount of data and detailed information contained in this paradigm-shifting book.

Johnathan possesses an uncommon blend of experiences as a former NFL player, attorney, civil rights advocate, and community, human services, and tech-based economic development executive. When combined with his experience as a leading economic competitiveness consultant, it becomes unequivocally clear that he is uniquely positioned to write what is sure to become the nation's winning economic playbook.

To my knowledge, there has never been a book written that encapsulates the economic challenges and opportunities of the nation through the lens of *economic inclusion and competitiveness* ideals. Johnathan has provided America a Rosetta Stone that will unlock and unleash untapped economic prowess, the dividends of which are immense and will over time provide a return on our national investment benefitting generations to come.

This book is a resource that is not to be read once and placed on a shelf. It introduces a new national economic narrative and imperative that should be studied and advanced through additional research and in media reports, consulting practices, comprehensive community economic development strategic plans, and course studies in institutions of higher learning. As essential as the army field manuals have been in the United States' previous armed conflicts, so will Johnathan's *The Future Economy and Inclusive Competitiveness* be in our current and future battle for global economic ascendency.

It is impossible to overstate the importance for leaders in government, education, and business to read this book, as well as anyone who is concerned about the future of our country. Without question, our national future embodies serious challenges. In *The Future Economy and Inclusive Competitiveness*, Johnathan shows us how we can go boldly and confidently into that future with our eyes squarely on the prize of shared and enduring prosperity.

Jay Williams
Former U.S. Assistant Secretary of Commerce for Economic Development
Administrator, Economic Development Administration
Washington, D.C.

DEDICATION

This book is dedicated to my . . .
Wife, Toni;
Mother, Vivian;
Family: The Campbells, Holifields, Jenkinses, and Prices;
Places: Romulus, MI; Morgantown, WV; Cincinnati, OH; Benton
Harbor, MI; Buffalo, NY; and Cleveland, OH; and
Friends: Known and unknown across our great nation.

ACKNOWLEDGEMENTS

"Gratitude makes sense of our past, brings peace for today and creates a vision for tomorrow."

~ *MELODY BEATTIE*

My grateful acknowledgement to the Kapor Center for Social Impact and John Carroll University for their sponsorship and to the West family for their contribution. Without their genuine interest and financial investment, it would have been impossible to fulfill this task.

The "soup-to-nuts" team at Let's Write Books, Inc. provided invaluable guidance in the writing, editing, proofreading, and graphic design processes. Their expertise, inspiration, professionalism, and coaching were indispensable to achieving my goal.

I also would like to express gratitude to my consultancy partners at ScaleUp Partners LLC and to my expanding national network of people, organizations, institutions, and governments who are embracing the demographic and geographic imperative of economic inclusion and competitiveness and are activating to address it.

A special thank you to my brother, David, whose persistent urging helped me "get off the dime."

Lastly, I humbly ask forgiveness of all those who have taken an interest in my vision and supported me over the years and whose names I have failed to mention.

TABLE OF CONTENTS

CHAPTER 1

INTRODUCTION

*"Entrepreneurship is the pursuit of opportunity
beyond resources currently controlled."*

– PROFESSOR HOWARD STEVENSON,
HARVARD BUSINESS SCHOOL

BRAVE NEW WORLD

Early in his tenure, President Barack Obama declared, "The United States can outcompete any other nation on earth."[1] His was an important statement, especially as it was made following a visit with President Hu Jintao of China, our number one economic rival. The president sent an unmistakable message not only to the world, but also to Americans: we *will* compete for global economic primacy.

Indeed, we live in an era of unprecedented economic opportunity unlike any we've ever seen before. Today, more jobs are possible, more access to economic success is within reach, and the ability to compete—and win—is actually a real possibility for those who desire it.

---

1   Sheryl Gay Stolberg, "Obama Urges U.S. Competitiveness Ahead of Speech," *The New York Times,* January 22, 2011, accessed July 28, 2015, http://www.nytimes.com/2011/01/23/us/politics/23radio.html?hp.

Moving away from outmoded economies has positioned more Americans to make meaningful contributions to our country and the world, all while reaping the economic benefits of those contributions.

At the same time, our world has become increasingly and uncompromisingly competitive, largely due to the accelerated globalization of the past generation. More and more, each one of us is being called upon to dig deep and muster the whole of our competitive spirit with a will to "show up" and do the best we can.

Unfortunately, not everyone is benefiting from this new paradigm. Not everyone is prospering. Our nation could be facing a future economic crisis due to the declines in traditional manufacturing, employment, and overall economic growth. In addition, our soon-to-be working population—children and youth—is shrinking while our aging population is exploding—and exiting the workforce as they retire. So, despite the fact that this era can open doors for more people than ever before and lead them to unprecedented economic success, it also has the potential to absolutely cripple and render helpless the economic prospects for America.

Why?

Two reasons: 1) the major shifts occurring within our population and 2) the invisibility of this era to those who are disconnected and unaware.

Based on census data, it is becoming abundantly clear that minority groups are growing at a faster rate than the White population. In fact, Brookings Institution demographer William Frey points out in "March of the Non-White Babies" that by 2042, "There will be no racial majority in the U.S. 'Minorities' ... will outnumber the White population."[2] Even today,

---

2   Tanvi Misra, "March of the Non-White Babies," *From the Atlantic, CityLab*, November 14, 2014, accessed August 4, 2015, http://www.citylab.com/housing/2014/11/march-of-the-non-white-babies/382576/.

we are seeing a large percentage of the population that is non-White. Specifically, 2015 U.S. Census data indicates that 13.3 percent and 17.6 percent of the total population in the U.S. is Black and Hispanic, respectively.[3] Because of this major demographic change, the economic torch is being passed from the White majority—who traditionally held economic positions of power—to a young, multicultural population. This shift does not stem from a sense of enlightenment or altruism from today's business leaders and moguls. Rather, it is the rapidly changing face of our nation that can thrust new demographic groups into positions of power—but only if these groups are ready and willing to capitalize on these unprecedented opportunities.

Taking advantage of these favorable circumstances must not be viewed as an option, but an imperative. If today's diverse youth fail to seize the reins of economic leadership in the future, we won't have enough contributors in this new economy. Frey concurs: "Because tomorrow's increasingly minority-driven youth and labor force population will be vital to maintaining a robust economy and to supporting a much more rapidly growing senior population, it is important to pay attention to the needs and opportunities available to the highly diverse post-millennial generation—not just in selected parts of the country, but everywhere."[4]

However, the exact population Frey mentions as vital to economic growth is found in disproportionately high numbers in disconnected communities—and on the whole, these are the communities that have not yet become high-level economic competitors. These so-called disconnected Americans lack awareness of the Innovation Economy:

---

3   "Quick Facts," United States Census Bureau, accessed August 20, 2015, https://www.census.gov/quickfacts/table/PST045215/00.

4   William H. Frey, "White aging means post-millennial America is becoming more diverse everywhere," *Brookings*, June 30, 2015, accessed August 5, 2015, http://www.brookings.edu/research/opinions/2015/06/30-white-aging-post-millennial-america-frey.

they are missing skills and competencies to access knowledge and resource networks. And they do not demonstrate education attainment and economic performance levels aligned with innovation-driven opportunities in entrepreneurship ecosystems, technology clusters, and emerging industry sectors. These disconnected populations comprise any groups that lag behind with respect to income, opportunity, and contributions to the national economy. By definition, this includes small-town and rural White populations, Blacks, Hispanics, and women. For example, women make up 51 percent of the U.S. population—yet their business receipts are less than 10 percent of the U.S. gross domestic product (GDP).[5] And while Black[6] and Hispanic[7] business ownership is on the rise, these businesses produce less than 1 percent and less than 3 percent, respectively, of the GDP.[8] An illustrative example of the point is that of the approximately 700,000 additional Black-owned businesses established between 2007 and 2012, only roughly 100,000 new jobs were generated.[9] This gives rise to another staggering fact: of the 2.6 million Black-owned businesses that exist, a whopping 2.5 million of them have *no* paid employees! Unemployment statistics are even more dire, with Black unemployment being approximately double that of the

5   "Fact Sheet: Women-Owned Businesses, NWBC Analysis of 2012 Survey of Business Owners," National Women's Business Council, accessed December 20, 2015, https://www.nwbc.gov/sites/default/files/Women%20Owned%20Businesses%20Fact%20Sheet.pdf.
6   Erika H. Becker-Medina, "Women are Leading the Rise of Black-Owned Businesses," U.S. Census Bureau, February 26, 2016, accessed December 21, 2016, http://blogs.census.gov/2016/02/26/women-are-leading-the-rise-of-black-owned-businesses/.
7   Robert Bernstein, "Hispanic-Owned Businesses on the Upswing," U.S. Census Bureau, December 1, 2016, accessed December 21, 2016, http://blogs.census.gov/2016/12/01/hispanic-owned-businesses-on-the-upswing/.
8   "World Bank national accounts data, and OECD National Accounts data files," World Bank Group, accessed December 21, 2016, http://data.worldbank.org/indicator/NY.GDP.MKTP.CD?locations=US.
9   "2012 Survey of Business Owners, Statistics for All U.S. Firms by Industry, Gender, Ethnicity, and Race for the U.S., States, Metro Areas, Counties, and Places: 2012," December 15, 2015, accessed December 20, 2015 http://factfinder.census.gov/faces/tableservices/jsf/pages/productview.xhtml?pid=SBO_2012_00CSA01&prodType=table.

White jobless rate. This has been a fairly constant relationship for more than forty consecutive years.[10] If half of the Black-owned businesses without employees grew to have just one, we'd add an impressive 1.25 million jobs to our economy.

Figures show these lower performing groups are growing. As Frey points out, "Racial minorities now account for all of the gains in the nation's children and younger labor force population; and by 2030 will account for all of its labor force gains."[11] By 2035, the "minority" non-White population for those under age twenty will have grown to 55 percent of the population (for its age group)—a clear majority.[12]

We appear to be experiencing the inexorable march of demography: the seemingly inevitable and unstoppable growth of disconnected populations. If they do in fact become the majority of Americans—a distinct possibility based on the numbers—yet are not positioned to make greater contributions, our economy is sure to falter.

Obviously, America cannot reach her highest economic competitiveness goals if so much of her population contributes so little. To include disconnected populations in the Innovation Economy is no longer a mere talking point or sound bite. It is absolutely imperative if America wants to retain her leadership seat at the global economic table.

At the same time, it is important to understand that my analysis is not meant to offend or denigrate any particular group of Americans. It

---

10   Derek Thompson, "The Workforce Is Even More Divided by Race Than You Think," *The Atlantic*, November 6, 2013, accessed December 20, 2015, http://www.theatlantic.com/business/archive/2013/11/the-workforce-is-even-more-divided-by-race-than-you-think/281175/.

11   William H. Frey, "State of the Union Positions Our Diverse Next Generation as a Domestic Policy Priority," *Brookings*, January 21, 2015, accessed August 5, 2015, http://www.brookings.edu/research/opinions/2015/01/21-state-of-the-union-diverse-next-generation-domestic-policy-priority-frey.

12   William H. Frey, "White aging means post-millennial America is becoming more diverse everywhere," *Brookings*, June 30, 2015, accessed August 5, 2015, http://www.brookings.edu/research/opinions/2015/06/30-white-aging-post-millennial-america-frey.

is my aim to shine a light on great areas of need and opportunity in our nation. I want to create a united awareness. For it is those disconnected communities who may suffer the most devastating effects if they do not become aware of, and connect with, this new economic era. It is with awareness that these historically disadvantaged groups will have greater prospects—and the choice and ability to be able to enter the primary economic game.

Why, then, are so many people unaware of this new economic age?

I believe we can answer this question by looking at the earlier economies that have characterized our nation's development. First we had the agrarian age, which was followed by the industrial age. Today, we have entered a third era, one that is much different from the earlier economies. It is the Innovation Economy.

The agrarian economy occurred from the early days of the colonies to the end of the nineteenth century. This economy relied on farming, and prosperity and opportunity were visible to any observer: it was easy to see what the farmer was doing, and the crops that he sold were the visible proof of his success.

The radical transformation of the economy from farming to manufacturing during the industrial era also had its own visible markers of productivity and success. It was quite easy to see the many men and women (and unfortunately, children) march daily into the manufacturing facilities of America, along with the enormous smokestacks dotting the nation's skylines in the Midwest to points east. Surely, it would have been difficult to miss the wealth of business leaders such as Andrew Carnegie and John D. Rockefeller, whose wealth was inextricably linked to industrial jobs creation and whose philanthropic contributions included the construction and establishment of public libraries throughout the U.S., Carnegie Hall, the University of Chicago, and the Rockefeller Institute for Medical Research.

The current age of the Innovation Economy is the economic period beginning with the late twentieth and early twenty-first centuries. It is marked by extreme socioeconomic changes brought about by unprecedented convergence of the globalization of commerce, democratization of information and technology, exponential growth of entrepreneurship, acceleration of new knowledge creation, and the interconnectedness of the world today. Many of those connected to and performing within the Innovation Economy are prospering to a degree that others may not even be able to imagine attaining. Not only are many in our country not joining in, contributing to, or benefiting from this new, promising era, there are others who are unaware of the existence of these new economic conditions.

It's not just the differences between the Innovation Economy and the industrial and agrarian ages that have made it difficult for some Americans to succeed. Rather, for many people—especially in disconnected communities—the Innovation Economy is a ghost, a nebulous apparition whose hallmarks of productivity, success, and prosperity are unrecognizable and markedly different from the previous two eras:

- There are no crops to grow, harvest, and sell. Instead, there are Petri dishes, beakers, volumetric flasks, and silicon chips.
- Scrubs, lab coats, and comfortable shoes have replaced a lot of hard hats, cranes, and construction boots.
- Instead of smokestacks, acid rain, and loud manufacturing equipment, there are seemingly quiet buildings that are artistically and architecturally pleasing to the eyes.
- Rather than financing businesses with secure bank loans, backed by borrowers' hard assets, there are angel investors and venture

capitalists who provide financing for startups and growing companies in exchange for a piece of those companies.

- Intellectual property, artificial intelligence, and virtual reality have become as important, or more important, than physical property.

Among the many phenomenal "success stories" are the unassuming yet brilliant tech giants like Jeff Bezos, Mark Zuckerberg, Steve Jobs, and Bill Gates rather than the traditional men in suits who command physically imposing "bricks and mortar" businesses with which the everyday man (or even disconnected American) can identify.

Without the evidence of production and prosperity that we are accustomed to seeing from the agrarian and industrial ages, it is easy to become, and stay, disconnected. In this age of the intangible, intellectual, and electronic-based product it is easy to be unaware of the drivers, even in areas that are home to our modern resources. With most of our innovation resources disproportionately located in large, urban areas, opportunity can be within reach of those who walk by those assets every day. Those oblivious to the industry and opportunity housed within those resources, or those who are geographically separated from these leading assets, need their curiosity triggered to ask and find answers to the question, "What's going on in those buildings?"

Fortunately, for those who do become curious ... for those who reach out ... for those who want to learn more ... the opportunities are limitless! This era has truly ushered in the opportunity for America to become, for the first time, a *truly inclusive* economy. And along with that, everyone—regardless of gender, race, color, or creed—can have as much chance of success as the next person. No longer will someone be shut out because of geography, finances, or lineage. Rather, this is the most egalitarian, democratic, and meritocratic economic period we've ever known. More than any other economic era, the Innovation Economy exemplifies these vital, economic opportunity-generating characteristics:

- Democratic because information is widely available like never before,
- Egalitarian because now "gray matter" is the determining factor, and
- Meritocratic because it is not based on an incumbent class privilege or wealth.

In these respects, and compared to previous major economies, the Innovation Economy is a marked improvement. It certainly is not a prefect embodiment of these ideals. However, it offers us substantially more and different opportunities waiting to be realized.

In addition to expanding opportunity beyond previous eras, it is necessary to expand opportunity *within* the Innovation Economy. That expansion will be accelerated by Inclusive Competitiveness® —an interdisciplinary framework to create community systems that improve the economic productivity and quality of life of disconnected Americans. In effect, we capitalize on the full and untapped potential of disconnected Americans to help fuel the economic vitality of the coming generations in ways that are more inclusive and durable. Inclusive Competitiveness® involves connecting minority, low-income, and other citizens to new opportunities that will benefit inner-city, urban, small town, and rural economies, and, ultimately, the national economy.

INTRODUCING
INCLUSIVE COMPETITIVENESS®

There is a major flaw in our current approach to national economic competitiveness. More than *not* sufficiently advancing people, my firm belief is that our nation's approach does not advance *enough* people. More people need to be involved. This book is about how we can set the stage for more contributions. Without intentionally focusing on broad inclusion, particularly of disconnected Americans, our current economic model will not grow enough new economic athletes—persons who demonstrate the skills mastery, agility, grit, and stamina to achieve sustained economic mobility, security, and prosperity, as well as life satisfaction—to maintain our global economic leadership.

Inclusive Competitiveness® is about intentionality—empowering new Americans with tools to reach up, grab hold, and pull down value from the national and global economy. The fundamentally unique premise of Inclusive Competitiveness®—and a reason why it was granted trademark status from the United States Patent and Trademark Office—is that for the first time it applies goals, objectives, metrics, strategies, policies, and expectations that advance U.S. economic competitiveness to new populations and communities (or to use my terminology, disconnected Americans). In this single brand, intellectual and emotional characteristics are conveyed about our nation's economic future and prospects for shared and enduring prosperity.

Inclusive Competitiveness® rewards are powerful and plentiful. By making the Innovation Economy accessible to disconnected citizens, we will begin to see:

- "New sources of human capital,"[13]
- Increased employment,
- Improved educational outcomes,
- Lower social welfare costs, and
- Legitimized "market processes by ensuring that outcomes are more broad-based and fair."[14]

As a result, the emerging Inclusive Competitiveness® Movement promises to create new economic athletes. These will be our stars, competitors who react to, and resiliently perform in, our volatile global economy in the same ways that winning sports athletes react to and perform in their respective unpredictable games. They can fill the dual pipelines of productivity to become higher impact, *intrapreneurial* employees–those who pursue opportunities to make valuable contributions to their employers' businesses–and higher growth *entrepreneurs* who create high-growth enterprises (HGEs). These are profitable, sustainable businesses that grow quickly and simultaneously create a disproportionately high number of new jobs. In fact, the Kauffman Foundation reveals in its report, *High-Growth Firms and the Future of the American Economy,* that "In any given year, the top-performing 1 percent of firms generates roughly 40 percent of new job creation."[15] Not surprisingly, HGEs will play a vital role in our current and future economy by increasing America's global economic competitiveness, resulting in new success and wealth. Interestingly, HGEs have a historical advantage on their side: the U.S. itself was conceived with an

---

13   Ibid.
14   Ibid.
15   Dane Stangler, "High-Growth Firms and the Future of the American Economy," *Ewing Marion Kauffman Foundation Research Series: Firm Formation and Economic Growth,* March 2010, 2, accessed August 8, 2015, http://www.kauffman.org/~/media/kauffman_org/research%20reports%20and%20covers/2010/04/high-growthfirmsstudy.pdf.

entrepreneurial mettle—not unlike an HGE. In the spirit of Professor Stevenson's definition of entrepreneurship, just as the colonists took a calculated risk to establish a new country by facing down the British Empire without regard to the resources they controlled, and won, HGEs are fearlessly taking on a challenging global economy ... and are winning as well. The philosophy that undergirds an HGE certainly is consistent with and reflects the best ethos of our nation's foundation, and this point should not be taken lightly.

However, our current roadmap to success won't be identical to the past. Land ownership and controlling production rights historically positioned someone for economic success and prosperity. Now, the Innovation Economy calls for less visible but much more attainable assets, such as brain power, creativity, and specialized talent. And even though there is more competition for jobs today than ever before, Inclusive Competitiveness® levels the playing field: you don't need to be rich, privileged, or politically connected, because everyone has gray matter and a contribution to make. To get the right answers we need to ask the right questions, open a narrative about the way forward, and most importantly, act. We can transform this "invisible" economy into one that is both visible and accessible to everyone. These are the first steps toward connecting with the Innovation Economy and achieving sustained national prosperity.

Martin Luther King, Jr. once said, "The arc of the moral universe is long, but it bends toward justice." In the same way, I believe that the arc of national economic competitiveness is long, but it bends toward Inclusive Competitiveness®.

But none of this happens instantaneously, especially when an economy is "invisible" to disconnected individuals and communities. I recall a leader of a student group once approached me after a presentation. He commented that the Black students in his group were still unaware of the Innovation Economy; that is, it was *invisible* to them. I encouraged this young man not to become discouraged and rather be patient—and in the meantime, act; get the word out by inculcating the message! I wanted him to share his passion and enthusiasm for this topic in the same way that I do. For if enough of us spread the word, eventually the message will not only become meaningful to everyone but will also ignite their motivation to take action and benefit from all the Innovation Economy has to offer.

SHATTERING GLASS CEILINGS ... AND MORE

At this point, you may be asking: "If what you say is true, what does this level of success look like?" Let's start with examples of "average" wealth in America: in 2011, the median figures for wealth holdings were $111,146 in White households, compared to just $7,113 for Black households and $8,348 for Hispanic households.[16] To highlight the point, in August 2016 it was estimated that if current policies remain in place, it will take two hundred and twenty-eight years (228 years!) for Blacks to accumulate the same amount of wealth Whites have now.[17] Importantly, with about one in ten workers (13 million people) being self-employed, U.S. entrepreneurs hold 37 percent of all wealth in the nation.[18]

---

16   Laura Sullivan, Tatjana Meschede, Lars Dietrich, & Thomas Shapiro ., "The Racial Wealth Gap," 2015, accessed August 4, 2015, http://www.demos.org/sites/default/files/publications/RacialWealthGap_1.pdf.

17   Kate Davidson, "It Would Take 228 Years for Black Families to Amass Wealth of White Families, Analysis Says," *The Wall Street Journal,* August 9, 2016, http://blogs.wsj.com/economics/2016/08/09/it-would-take-228-years-for-black-families-to-amass-wealth-of-white-families-analysis-says/.

18   "Including People of Color in the Promise of Entrepreneurship," An Educational Policy Brief From the Ewing Marion Kauffman Foundation, December 5, 2016, http://www.kauffman.org/~/media/kauffman_org/resources/2016/including%20people%20of%20color%20in%20the%20promise%20of%20entrepreneurship%20pdf.pdf.

For all such homes to simply have that "average" wealth level would be positively transformative. Think about the possibilities for greater prosperity for each of the nearly 10 million Black households[19] and about 12 million Hispanic households[20] that would occur with more than $100,000 of additional wealth holdings. This equates to about $1 trillion more wealth holdings for Blacks and nearly $1.2 trillion more wealth holdings for Hispanics.

Now, let's go one step further: What if we could get disconnected populations to *surpass* the average? We would no doubt witness explosive economic growth and prosperity. A good analogy for this can be seen with the Rogers innovation curve (see Figure 1).

This curve, originally published in 1962, illustrates the diffusion of technology in a given population. As you can see, when any new innovation is introduced, there is a small percentage (approximately 2.5 percent) of actual innovators. These are the creators, the initial movers and shakers. Next, there is a slightly larger group (13.5 percent) of "early adopters" who early on in the cycle get on board with the new technologies. Eventually, the majority of the population follows suit, with only a small group of "laggards" hanging behind.

---

19 "African Americans by the Numbers," accessed August 4, 2015, http://www.infoplease.com/spot/bhmcensus1.htm
20 "Hispanic Americans by the Numbers," accessed August 4, 2015, http://www.infoplease.com/spot/hhmcensus1.html

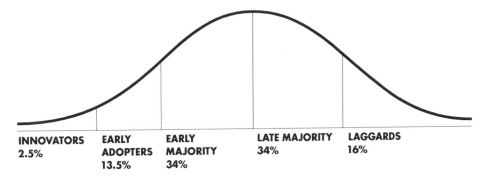

| INNOVATORS 2.5% | EARLY ADOPTERS 13.5% | EARLY MAJORITY 34% | LATE MAJORITY 34% | LAGGARDS 16% |

Figure 1. Diffusion of ideas. Adapted from *Wikipedia Commons*, by Tungsten, 2009, retrieved August 1, 2015, from https://commons.wikimedia.org/wiki/File:Diffusionofideas.PNG. Adapted with permission.

Sumesh Arora, in his article, "Innovation in Mississippi Must Be Inclusive," makes the case for nurturing a "culture of innovation" to motivate people to become the true innovators, or "game changers."[21]

He points out that using this curve and taking into account population numbers will allow us to see the powerful potential for innovation throughout our society. For instance, if you apply those percentages to the entire population of disconnected Americans, it becomes evident just how many potentially groundbreaking innovators may not be currently connecting with the best opportunities. Look at what we could be missing as a nation:

- 2.5 percent of the 41 million Blacks in the U.S.[22] would equate to over a million potential innovators who could be adding greater value to our nation.

---

21 Sumesh Arora, "Innovation in Mississippi must be inclusive," *Mississippi Business Journal,* June 26, 2015, accessed August 4, 2015, http://msbusiness.com/2015/06/sumesh-arora-innovation-in-mississippi-must-be-inclusive/.

22 "African American Population Growth," 2013, accessed August 5, 2015, http://blackdemographics.com/population/.

- With 54 million Hispanics[23] in the U.S., 2.5 percent would mean approximately 1.35 million new innovators who could create change, new businesses, and new technologies.

- About 2.5 million women could become innovators when you consider the 100 million non-Hispanic White women living in the U.S.

- About 81 percent of the nation is urban,[24] but 19.3 percent of the population lives in rural areas, which means there could be another 1.5 million creators/innovators among those groups.

This curve has empirical validity and has withstood the test of time for now over fifty years. It demonstrates that *millions* of Americans could be contributing and leading in exponential ways—if only they were better connected to our best opportunities.

So ... what if every state's traditionally disconnected populations began to join this movement of innovation? The number of disconnected people would begin to shrink as those same people become the innovation creators and early adopters in the nation and the world. Not only would this be an advantage to the individuals themselves but also to the growth of the nation's businesses, jobs, and wealth, effectively benefiting their communities and the overall economy.

A CALL TO ACTION

Clearly, these changes won't occur magically or even organically. So far, disconnected populations are missing out. But if we can empower individuals and equip them with the tools and a new economic narrative and vision, then anything is possible. Up until now, disconnected

---

23 "Hispanic or Latino Populations," May 5, 2015, accessed August 5, 2015, http://www.cdc.gov/minorityhealth/populations/REMP/hispanic.html.
24 "2010 Census Urban Area Facts," 2010, accessed August 5, 2015, https://www.census.gov/geo/reference/ua/uafacts.html.

communities and individuals simply have not been offered these opportunities—nor have they demanded them. For them, as mentioned earlier, this exciting economy has been all but visible.

Thirty years ago, we couldn't imagine paying four dollars for a fancy cup of coffee. Today, we sit in the Starbucks' drive-through and demand our Venti cappuccinos! Thirty years ago, we would laugh if someone wanted to sell us a three-dollar liter of water. Today, we tote bottles of Fiji and VOSS to the gym, and no one thinks twice about it. In both examples, we as consumers were *offered* an innovation—something new—and we adopted it. Similarly, it's time we start *offering* Innovation Economy opportunities to *all* Americans.

And just as important, now is the time for disconnected communities to meet new economic offerings by not just wishing for, but *demanding* a piece of the innovation pie!

Remember, though, identifying economic success is a challenge in this era. Years ago, it was easy to spot prosperity. I grew up west of Detroit in Romulus, Michigan. As with many other families, mine was, and continues to be, a direct beneficiary of the industrial economy. As part of the first Great Migration, in 1920 my grandparents arrived in Detroit from Tuskegee, Alabama and Chattanooga, Tennessee. Since then, for nearly a hundred years, my family has worked for the Ford Motor Company. During my childhood, I drove by the factories, witnessed uncles and cousins head off to work in the plants, and heard all about Ford's and others' industrial might. Today, however, it is e-mail and social media, research and commercialization, private capital and angel investor networks—as opposed to the rather physical and obvious displays of economic strength in the industrial era. These success markers may be invisible to those who don't know they exist. Therefore, we must begin to engage all Americans. How? By making them aware of, and getting them excited about, new opportunities and pointing out indicators of success consistent with this new economic era. When this happens—as it did with the vocational education and training thrust that was nationally launched in the 1960s—more people will demand access to the education, training, networks, and technical tools they need to enter, and thrive within, the Innovation Economy.

Interestingly, turning things around won't spontaneously begin with only the innovators. Surely, innovators are a necessary part of the equation, but it's those "early enablers" in the form of policymakers who hold a very important key. They are the catalysts for a new economic policy regime that can create favorable conditions to improve Innovation Economy connectivity. Together, these leading-edge players will be the stimulus for growing an economy that has the potential to become more robust and inclusive than ever.

WHO THIS BOOK IS FOR

This book is about the economic inclusion and competitiveness of disconnected Americans, the communities in which they live, and shared prosperity. I adopt the U.S. Department of Commerce's Economic Development Administration's (EDA) definition of the role of economic development: "[Creating] the *conditions* for economic growth and improved quality of life by expanding the capacity of individuals, firms, and communities to maximize the use of their talents and skills to support innovation, lower transaction costs, and responsibly produce and trade valuable goods and services[emphasis added]."[25] The "conditions" described by EDA begin with new community systems, requiring "effective, collaborative institutions focused on advancing mutual gain

---

25 "What is Economic Development?" U.S. Department of Commerce, Economic Development Administration, accessed November 28, 2016, https://www.eda.gov/.

for the public and the private sector,"[26] to reasonably, reliably, and predictably produce the desired outcomes of "economic growth and improved quality of life" in disconnected communities.

As such, and in the broadest of terms, this book is for *anyone*, and not just for a select audience of "technical" readers. It is for anyone who cares about our country's growth and development: ordinary Americans, business leaders, entrepreneurs, innovators, people who work with today's youth (tomorrow's global economic athletes), and anyone else concerned with our economic future. This book is also designed to inspire and invite those in positions of influence, including and beyond political leaders, to affect and create a new Inclusive Competitiveness® policy regime. This includes leaders of economic development organizations, community organizers, philanthropists, elected and appointed government officials (at the national, state, and local levels), and education leaders—basically, any influencer connected to innovation, economy, and the community.

The policymakers are so important because, without them, the paradigm shift cannot be made: the systems can't be put in place to support Inclusive Competitiveness®, and building the necessary momentum to achieve and sustain broad prosperity in the Innovation Economy will not be possible. My definition of policy is the influential actors' expression of important public objectives. Policies are foundational to the change we need, because meaningful investment never precedes policy. Never. And if you want a new result in the marketplace—such as igniting a National Inclusive Competitiveness® Movement—you had better tell the market it is important and provide some resources for the change to happen.

---

26   Ibid.

Programs come and go, but the strategy (policy) is the North Star, and that is what endures. But right now, if you look across the U.S. at our actions so far, there is no national policy; no inclusive North Star focused on where we, as a diverse nation, want to play; no sustained effort to create new community systems to improve the productivity of disconnected Americans in today's Innovation Economy. Without a guiding light via policy, programs become disjointed pieces of a puzzle that never truly fit together in support of an overarching national goal–that of building an innovative, sustainable, flourishing economy that improves lives, and elevates the U.S. to an even higher level of global economic prominence.

The missing element is the full conversation around economic inclusion and competitiveness. Now more than ever, we need a new narrative–a new, national conversation in which everyone contributes and participates, including those in disconnected communities.

We all talk with each other about things that we believe are important. However, as Americans we rarely talk about the cornerstones of the Innovation Economy, inclusion and competitiveness–even though our present and future prosperity depends on them. It is incumbent upon us, then, to catalyze and infuse this important conversation into our families, communities, institutions, and organizations–and this new narrative must begin with those in a position to impact policy.

Therefore, if policymakers (and influencers) begin to consider and embrace the concepts outlined in this book, we will be able to leverage unprecedented power that elevates and propels our disconnected citizens to become successful, prosperous contributors and leaders in this new economic era. The end result will be more innovations, better lives, more businesses and jobs, and more wealth for *everyone.*

It is my hope that this book will spark a revolution of minds so that we may create the necessary narratives and polices both for those who are ready to capitalize on the many exciting opportunities this era has to offer and those who have yet to become aware of the Innovation Economy. This is essential for every individual as well as the economic future of our country.

USE OF INCLUSIVE COMPETITIVENESS® AND THE INCLUSIVE COMPETITIVENESS® FRAMEWORK IN THIS BOOK

For the sake of clarity and simplicity, for the balance of this book, Inclusive Competitiveness® is used within the text as *Inclusive Competitiveness* and the Inclusive Competitiveness® Framework is used as the *IC Framework*.

CHAPTER 2

FROM THE NFL TO THE NEW ECONOMY

A COMPETITOR'S JOURNEY

EPIPHANY

Merriam-Webster defines an epiphany "as a moment in which you suddenly see or understand something in a new or very clear way." For me, *Inclusive Competitiveness* was an epiphany.

Notably, in their truest sense, epiphanies do not manifest out of nothingness. They are the breakthroughs that can occur after considerable thought, experience, and reflection. A great example of this is Gordon Gould's description of the epiphany that led to the invention of the laser:

> In the middle of one Saturday night ... the whole thing
> ... suddenly popped into my head and I saw how to build
> the laser ... but that flash of insight required the 20 years

of work I had done in physics and optics to put all of the bricks of that invention in there.

In other words, an epiphany can be viewed as simply the final piece of a complex puzzle falling into place.[27] Often epiphanies are triggered by a new and key piece of information, but importantly, a depth of prior knowledge is required to allow the leap of understanding.[28]

Similarly, my career path, which led to the development of the twenty-first century imperative of *Inclusive Competitiveness,* has been a highly informative and eclectic journey. Along the way, I've developed a deep sense of purpose and my perspective on matters of economic inclusion and competitiveness has grown authentically, organically, and, even sometimes, painfully. So that you can have a clear understanding of how and why these concepts were created, the following pages share my unique background, career path, and relevant experiences.

JUDGE'S VERDICT

"Johnathan, you're an iconoclast!" In an unmistakably distinctive, baritone voice, those were the words spoken to me by the Honorable William A. McClain, affectionately known as "Judge." He was both a friend and mentor who also had a reputation for breaking barriers. Living to an impressive 101 years of age, this man was:

- The first Black member of the Cincinnati Bar Association,
- The first Black attorney to serve as city solicitor (lead attorney) of any major city in the country,

---

27 Scott Berkun, *The Myths of Innovation*, O'Reilly Media, Sebastopol, CA, 1 edition, 2010, 9-10.
28 Duco A. Schreuder, *Vision and Visual Perception: The Conscious Base of Seeing*, Archway Publishing, Bloomington, IN, 2014, 671.

- A founder of the Progressive Black Masonry Movement as a 33rd degree Mason[29] (a high ranking position), and
- National president of Sigma Pi Phi Fraternity (commonly known as the Boulé), the nation's first Greek-letter organization comprised primarily of Black men

... and this is just to name a few of his accomplishments!

After having looked up the definition of iconoclast, I discovered that Judge had indeed paid me a great compliment. This influential and awe-inspiring man was acknowledging my spirit when it came to challenging widely held and accepted beliefs and practices.

I have never been one to accept the status quo or conventional wisdom. Rather, my driving passion is to make the contribution I am uniquely poised to make—no matter the cost—and this defines the way I live my life. That Judge saw integrity of purpose and passion in me years ago makes me proud, indeed.

This contrarian nature has, at times, landed me in some hot water, as you'll see throughout this chapter. Still, my continuing pursuit of constant improvement and to make a substantive difference at all levels has allowed me to forge my own path and win in situations that I was "supposed" to lose. It is my belief that to inspire enduring change, you must see situations differently. You need to look for the potential in people and situations that others might miss—and then help bring that potential to the surface. Looking back, I see that common thread—that pioneering, entrepreneurial spirit has been with me throughout my life—motivating me, even early in my childhood.

And it's why on my office wall hangs the following quote, which has such deep personal meaning for me:

---

29 "William A. McClain," Cincinnati History Library and Archives, accessed August 24, 2015, http://library.cincymuseum.org/aag/bio/mcclain.html.

And it ought to be remembered that there is nothing more difficult to take in hand, more perilous to conduct, or more uncertain in its success, than to take the lead in the introduction of a new order of things. Because the innovator has for enemies all those who have done well under the old conditions, and lukewarm defenders in those who may do well under the new.

-MACHIAVELLI, THE PRINCE

EARLY INFLUENCES

On January 8, 1964, Lyndon B. Johnson declared a "War on Poverty" to combat the nation's high poverty rate during that era. This led to the passage of bipartisan legislation through the Economic Opportunity Act of 1964. Many programs and initiatives resulted from this legislation, including Food Stamps (now known as SNAP), the Peace Corps, Medicare and Medicaid, Head Start, and the expansion of Social Security, just to name a few.[30] Being born later that same year, I sometimes find it interesting that, more than fifty years hence, I have committed my life to some of the same "War on Poverty" issues to help affect and shape our country's economic future. And although politicians will debate the success or failure of these programs—both past and present—one fact cannot be ignored, regardless of political leanings: no matter the era and no matter the actions that are taken, the economy is of primary importance in the global competition for success as a nation.

Of course, early on I was more focused on the typical concerns of childhood—namely family, friends, school, and sports. Football, in

---

30 Melissa Boteach, Erik Stegman, Sarah Baron, Tracey Ross, and Katie Wright, , "The War on Poverty: Then and Now," January 7, 2014, accessed August 31, 2015, https://www.americanprogress.org/issues/poverty/report/2014/01/07/81661/the-war-on-poverty-then-and-now/.

particular, became a passion of mine. Yet at the same time, some of my early role models predicted some of my later interests. I looked up to people like my grandfather, the Reverend Lieutenant Beecher Campbell, Sr., a Baptist preacher in whose home I was reared. Back then national figures like O.J. Simpson (long before his criminal trials) and Jesse Jackson also appealed to me. During the 1970s I saw the positive mark they were making on society through their drive, enthusiasm, charisma, and commitment. Deep faith, athletic prowess, and civil rights activism became profoundly embedded in what I valued at the time—and still value to this day.

GAME CHANGERS

In high school, I began to realize some of those leadership aspirations when I became captain of the Romulus High School football team, located in Metro Detroit. This team was not good. In fact, our record was a dismal 0-9, with one particular debacle ending in a 64-point shutout defeat! One well-meaning physical education teacher told me to forget my dreams of Division I football (now the Football Bowl Subdivision). Instead, he told me I should attend local Wayne State University and be content with being "a big fish in a small pond" rather than trying to join a nationally competitive football program only to become "a small fish in a big pond." In the typical fiery style of my youth, I shot back, "How about I become a *big* fish in a *big* pond?" I didn't let the advice of teachers and friends dissuade or distract me. I started out as a walk-on for West Virginia University's football team under College Football Hall of Fame coach Don Nehlen; I earned a scholarship in one semester, became a starter by sophomore year, and was elected captain by teammates my senior year. Coach Nehlen has shared with me that

I "may have been [his] number-one success story." That's a humbling tribute from a Hall of Fame coach.

All of this happened despite having no money, no connections, and little material support. In essence, this was the beginning of my personal entrepreneurial journey. In fact, on January 5, 1983, I stood at the Detroit Greyhound Station with my mother. She said she planned to buy me a round-trip ticket to West Virginia University and back—just in case things didn't work out. My response? "Thanks, Ma, but I'm getting a one-way ticket. I'm not coming home until I'm supposed to."

I had clear intention, the prayers of friends and family, and an unshakable belief that I could compete and win—and this is what allowed me to capitalize on opportunities, even without what most people would consider the "necessary" resources. I knew that I wanted to contribute in a big way to a major program. I wasn't going to settle for those either/ or options that were presented to me. Instead, I charted my own path, and that attitude animates everything I do.

The path was not always a smooth one. During my junior year, I got in some trouble one evening during a big, off-campus bar fight. The incident involved several of my Black teammates and White club-owners and bouncers and was explicitly racial. It resulted in felony and misdemeanor charges for me, as well as other players, but none for the owners or bouncers. I ended up with more charges than anybody else despite my marginal involvement. So, I found a lawyer from the NAACP in West Virginia to represent me.

At first, I was embarrassed to be associated with the publicity surrounding that incident. But after weeks of seeing my name and face plastered all over places like *ESPN* and *USA Today*, I became so disgusted by all of it that I finally said, "This is not who I am. *This will not define me. I will define myself!*"

In the end, after telling my story to the grand jury, I was not indicted (nor were any of my teammates) and all charges were dropped. It was learning how to bounce back from embarrassment and ridicule that taught me invaluable lessons in overcoming hardships and difficult challenges. Even with the charges still pending, my self-belief allowed me to rise above the surrounding negativity when, at the time, I ran for the Student Administration's Board of Governors ... and won a seat!

After the unfortunate incident was over, the university vice president of Student Affairs took me to lunch. Surprisingly, he told me that the chief of police did not believe that I was a main culprit in the fight, but he thought that by keeping the heat on me I would feel compelled to give the police and prosecutor more information. According to the VP, the chief "respected me" for turning around my situation and becoming a student leader. As much as I appreciated the concession, the lessons I learned and the leadership skills I gained throughout the case were much more valuable. Learning the motivations for "overcharging" me definitely helped firmly steer me toward a career that focuses on civil rights and policy issues. That realization and my time spent working closely with the NAACP lawyer were both defining experiences that would serve me well in the future and continue to do so now.

Even though I was fortunate enough to be drafted by the NFL's Cincinnati Bengals in 1987, I was cut from the team during preseason. So I returned to school to finish my degree and ran track to stay in condition to make another run at the NFL. In an interesting turn of events that year, the players went on strike and NFL owners continued to play games with "replacement" players. The call from the Bengals to join the replacement team at that time meant a difficult choice: either join the "scabs" and continue my dream of an NFL career or stay in school to finish my degree—and risk losing the opportunity forever.

Though the decision was a difficult one, and perhaps underpinned by my upbringing in a union family, I did refuse the offer. I explained that I would not join the replacement players because I wanted to complete my degree, yet I made it clear that I still had a deep interest in joining the team the following year. It was important to me to have a chance to walk through the front door—not the "scab" backdoor—and compete straight up to win a roster spot.

Just a few months later the Bengals called back to offer me a free agent contract for the following year. Without hesitation or negotiation, I accepted.

An injury in 1988 meant I could practice, but not play, the entire season, nor could I compete in the Super Bowl. I bounced back from that broken leg and returned the following year to become the surprise of training camp. Unfortunately, an injury-free season was not part of my future. Despite making the team, a knee injury in 1989 forced me out of action for most of that season, too, and my NFL career ended the following year.

Despite those setbacks, the experience was an extraordinary one. In fact, I often tell people—playfully, of course—that while I was on the team, the Bengals were one of the NFL's best. And when they cut me in 1990, the team went fourteen consecutive years without a winning record—a clear cause and effect!

Another good friend and mentor, Judge John West, had an insight I will never forget. During lunch one day, he said, "Johnathan, you got out of that game just in time." He continued, "Your career with the Bengals was so short that you had little choice but to go back to school and prepare for the rest of your life. You didn't stay long enough to earn any real money. Had you stayed a few more years, your perspective likely would have been far different. Instead of thinking you were 'owed' something, you got to work on building the rest of your life."

Those words resonated with me. No doubt I was deeply disappointed and angry when I was released from the team. However, I was not destined to have a long career in the NFL; the truth was, I simply wasn't good enough. I was eking by, barely holding onto a roster spot. As Judge West said, I didn't have a choice at that point. I knew nothing was owed to me and that no one was handing out opportunities. I realized that if I was going to enjoy the kind of life I wanted, I had to prepare and compete hard for it. If nothing else, I was a competitor.

A few months after my football career ended, I enrolled in graduate school at the University of Cincinnati. I earned a master's in education but eventually took a slightly different turn by pursuing law school; in my mind, the Juris Doctor was simply going to be more flexible and marketable throughout my career.

During law school, I made conscious efforts to accelerate my community contributions. It was then that I reached out to Dr. Milton Hinton, recently retired University of Cincinnati professor of education and vice provost, who just had been elected president of the city's NAACP. I left a voice message for Dr. Hinton saying that I was interested in working with him, especially in the area of fundraising. NAACP branches (or chapters) are chronically under-resourced and I thought that by expressing interest in raising funds, I would get the new president's attention.

Dr. Hinton called me back and said, "Young man, you are in law school. Don't you think that's your priority? Just take care of that and then we'll talk." I told him I could and wanted to do both. He reluctantly accepted my offer of support and we became fast friends. Dr. Hinton was a seminal mentor who knew that I needed opportunities to mature as a leader and advocate. Showing confidence in me, he provided meaningful assignments (in spades) that helped me grow. Working with the Cincinnati NAACP on a wide range of matters—including minority business contracting, police-community relations, housing discrimination, and government and education reform—was close to having a full-time job. Under Dr. Hinton's leadership, we made meaningful contributions to the community. What's more, he was committed to helping me fulfill my potential and he continues to be a great friend and mentor.

After graduating from University of Cincinnati College of Law, I began my first job as an assistant prosecutor for Hamilton County, Ohio. While being a Black prosecutor in this locality was not common, being a Black *civil, rather than criminal,* prosecuting attorney was even more rare. My tenure with the prosecutor's office benefited me greatly. With the practice's emphasis on civil rights, I had a chance to immerse myself in state and federal civil rights law from the government's perspective, rather than through the lens of an activist.

Within a couple of years, I moved into a smaller private practice in the city of Cincinnati and increased my community activity, focusing on civil rights, economic development, and government and educational reforms. A highlight of my legal career was serving as lead counsel for the Cincinnati NAACP[31] in a redlining, housing-discrimination lawsuit against Nationwide Insurance. During that time, I had the opportunity to travel to Richmond, Virginia for a few days. The purpose of my trip was to observe and receive guidance from Tim Kaine—2016 vice presidential nominee—who was lead counsel against the same insurance company for refusing to provide insurance to Black homeowners in majority-Black areas.

---

31 "HOME of Cincinnati settles with Nationwide for $1.25 Million," National Fair Housing Advocate Online, accessed November 28, 2016, http://www.fairhousing.com/index.cfm?method=page.display&pagename=releases_cinci-home-2-26-99.

Some of my community activities were at odds with some of the city's incumbent civic leaders—including the local chamber of commerce. Even though we did not always see eye to eye—and most times my "side" prevailed on the issues—I was still able to develop a good rapport with the chamber CEO.

It was during that time that I received an important phone call—a phone call that changed my life.

A CALL FROM THE CHAMBER

Chambers of commerce are historically conservative. They generally have been associated with political conservatism and maintaining the status quo. Certainly, they are not bastions of progressivism—and yet, I received a most unexpected phone call.

The call went something like this: "Would you be interested in helping the chamber of commerce figure out what it wants to do in the New Economy?"

There was nothing in my background that would have predicted that call. I was not your typical White, conservative businessman (most common in the membership and staff at the local chamber). I had not worked at a large, prestigious law firm and I was not an up-and-coming brand manager for Procter & Gamble. Instead, I was in a relatively small firm at the time in Cincinnati and active in sometimes contentious civic and political affairs.

The gentleman to whom I spoke that day was John Williams, the long-time president and CEO of the Greater Cincinnati Chamber of Commerce. While he viewed me as a promising young lawyer with a lot of passion and potential, I had little background in technology and innovation and was therefore not an ideal candidate on paper. But when asked by the press why he selected me to lead the chamber's

New Economy initiatives, Williams quipped, "Who better than a running back? This is not a well-choreographed play. This is a broken play. And you've got to get that first down, [so] you go figure out how the hell to do it."[32] At the chamber, I was afforded a rare opportunity and platform to gain new perspective to have lasting impact on the community at a grassroots level.

I was accustomed to working with traditional organizations that offered singularly direct-service and place-based programs to the local community. These are services delivered directly to individuals and families that are designed to help people avoid long-term problems, decrease their risk for crisis situations, and enhance their chances of leading productive, satisfying lives. Examples include early childhood education; parent and youth development; job training, readiness, development, and placement; small business technical assistance and education; and formerly incarcerated and reentry programs.

These organizations are both vital and integral components to any community and can make a profound difference in people's lives. However, what they often lack is the exponential impact that comes with other systems-focused entities that are discussed in this book. This is why I make the distinction between direct-service and place-based programs and community systems. When it comes to economic opportunity, many funders and advocates look for justification for continued funding on a superficial cause-effect level. Often, they laud a single exceptional program or individual outcome in a disconnected community that is the product of extraordinary labor or other special circumstances. But in their excitement about these exceptions, they generally miss the bigger picture. The questions they really need to ask

---

32 John Byczkowski, "New economy: Non-techie to lead tech initiative," *The Enquirer*, May 7, 2000, accessed August 16, 2015, http://www.enquirer.com/editions/2000/05/07/fin_new_economy.html.

are these: How can we throw the net wider? Are there systems that we can create to support this work, and therefore increase the probability that more of these positive outcomes will occur over time?

While I knew we were making meaningful contributions to citizens with direct-service and place-based programs, I was regularly frustrated that we couldn't have broader, more sustainable reach and impact. This feeling became even more pronounced when I was given the chance to peek over to the other side of the community economic playing field in my new position as vice president of New Economy Enterprise at the chamber.[33] It was clear as day that the game being played among top economic performers was "major league." Coming from a community development and civil rights background, I realized that the disconnected populations were playing in the economic "minor leagues"–and not because they didn't want to compete and contribute at the highest level. They simply had neither an idea how nor support to break into the "big game."

One initiative that I led with the chamber was the formation of CincyTech, an organization focused on developing the Innovation Economy of Cincinnati through workforce and education development, policy and advocacy leadership, supporting research and commercialization, and making resources available for entrepreneurs and young companies. Once CincyTech was formed, I assumed responsibility as the founding executive director (possibly the first and only Black person in the U.S. to lead a regional technology and innovation economic development initiative) and continued my role as vice president for the chamber. My overall vision at CincyTech was to build and lead an organization that would steward the broadly defined Innovation

---

33   John J. Byczkowski, "Lawyer leads tech effort: Chamber taps Holifield for new position," *The Cincinnati Enquirer,* May 3, 2000, accessed November 29, 2016, http://www.enquirer.com/editions/2000/05/03/fin_lawyer_leads_tech.html.

Economy through venture development, education, entrepreneurship, and workforce and policy solutions.

Accordingly, we started by working with a corporate partner, Cincinnati Bell, and Cincinnati Public Schools to create the first information technology-focused high school in the state of Ohio: Robert A. Taft Information Technology High School.[34] With the local community college, Cincinnati State, we were able to acquire a donation of technology equipment from EDS (Electronic Data Systems), valued at nearly eight million dollars, for a new Advanced Technology and Learning Center.[35] We also worked to create entrepreneurship resources during that time. Among those was the Tri-State Growth Capital Fund: a $40 million venture capital fund[36] and a truly significant accomplishment!

I have always believed that a broad-based approach is the only way to achieve sustained regional economic prosperity. This approach includes, among other things, a focus on higher growth entrepreneurship, education, public and private sector policy, and workforce development. Other key stakeholders and the new chamber CEO were interested in focusing solely on higher growth entrepreneurship. Despite our early triumphs, and that we both wanted to create enduring economic success for the region, our differing "means to an end" meant that I was not aligned with the vision of leading stakeholders. So we mutually agreed to part ways.[37]

---

34 "Team effort will create 'Tech High,'" *ChamberVision*, Volume 43, Issue 5, August 2001, accessed November 29, 2016, https://www.cincinnatichamber.com/uploadedFiles/chamber/Pages/News/Connect/cv0108.pdf.

35 Kristina Goetz, "College halfway to goal of $16M: Cincinnati State only 7 weeks into 4-year financial campaign," *The Cincinnati Enquirer*, July 2, 2002, accessed November 29, 2016, http://enquirer.com/editions/2002/07/02/loc_college_halfway_to.html.

36 James McNair, "New capital fund raises $40 million," *The Cincinnati Enquirer*, March 27, 2003, accessed November 29, 2016, http://enquirer.com/editions/2003/03/27/biz_buzz27.html.

37 Lance Williams, "Holifield resigns from CincyTechUSA," *Cincinnati Business Courier*, April 5, 2004, accessed November 29, 2016, http://www.bizjournals.com/cincinnati/stories/2004/04/05/daily7.html.

THE HARBOR SHORES PROJECT

After CincyTech, I took a position in Benton Harbor, Michigan. This is one of the nation's lowest economically performing cities, and I believed I could have some impact there. During my time in Michigan, I was the executive vice president of a relatively new organization called the Council for World Class Communities.

During my one year there I was able to contribute to a promising development project called Harbor Shores. This was a project designed to bridge the communities of Benton Harbor and St. Joseph. Although geographically situated next to one another, separated only by the St. Joseph River, there was a socioeconomic chasm: Benton Harbor was more than 90 percent Black with a high poverty rate, while St. Joseph was about 90 percent White with a low poverty rate. Any improvement in relations between Benton Harbor and St. Joseph could only take place within the context of a broader community economic development movement.

The Harbor Shores project (situated about ninety miles from downtown Chicago) outlined a plan to develop approximately 1,000 middle- and upper-income new second homes for the Chicago market. Those plans included a Jack Nicklaus signature golf course, a water park, units of low- and moderate-income housing, as well as office, retail, and green space. The scale and magnitude of Harbor Shores—a $500 million land development project—had the potential to be transformational for not only Benton Harbor but also the other two impacted communities of St. Joseph and Benton Township. The Harbor Shores development represented a whopping $13,700 per capita investment for the total population of 33,000 from all three impacted communities. Moreover, the projected total economic impact was expected to accrue $630 million in the first seven years as a result of new wealth from job creation and spending. The overarching vision was that Benton Harbor would also become a prosperous hub for recreation, hospitality, and travel in Southwest Michigan.

The widespread implications were only limited by imagination. Benton Harbor is a small community, so what if we achieved the same scale of economic investment in a large city like Chicago? Relatively speaking, that would equate to a huge *$50 billion* project to get that same level of per capita investment. Thinking on those terms, I could appreciate the unique opportunity of this project. Benton Harbor was presented a (perhaps) once-in-a-lifetime shot to transform itself, and it would need more than temporary "job creation" to optimize the project's impact and help ensure Benton Harbor's economic sustainability. We would need to create a multi-pronged plan to leverage the project's initial new jobs, implementing programs and strategic initiatives focused on homeownership, workforce solutions, education and literacy, community ventures development, arts and culture consortiums, and more. In my mind, the sky was the limit!

At the time I developed a plan called "Three Phases of Equitable Community Transformation" that encapsulated my thinking. In essence, it was a community benefits plan for the Harbor Shores project that would operate in three phases. It would effectively help the city to build its capacity to become an interdependent community in relation to St. Joseph instead of being dependent. Each phase would leverage the success of earlier phases, and because this plan dealt with the near- and long-terms, there would be opportunity for community growth and development long after jobs created in the project's initial construction phase were no longer needed.

However, my contrarian approach did put me at loggerheads with the powers leading Harbor Shores, which caused a rift similar to that with CincyTech.

At the time, Whirlpool Corporation was the main funding source for both the Harbor Shores project and my organization, which meant they dictated much of the direction the effort took. I was focused on the community development side of the equation and this did not fit with their preferred approach. The corporate executives wanted to zero in on diversity training and export their corporate diversity training model to the Benton Harbor and St. Joseph communities.

The problem, as I saw it, was that Whirlpool employees had jobs, benefits, 401(k)s, etc. In other words, everyone involved in their successful corporate diversity training was generally independent. Building capacity to move the company from a state of individualized independence toward greater diversity, inclusion, and the desired state of organizational interdependence was not a huge stretch: it was certainly attainable. But that approach would not best serve the people of Benton Harbor. The community was in a much more dependent position, with a poverty rate approaching 50 percent and a college graduation rate of less than 5 percent. Benton Harbor was a subsidized community, unable to even marginally—let alone optimally—exist without outside assistance and direction from others. To expect a community that is accustomed to being dependent on others to suddenly make a great leap over to a mindset of interdependence—without first achieving a measure of independence—was asking too much. But such was the prevailing paradigm.

The rift would remain as long as I stayed in Benton Harbor. Despite the adoption of key elements of my community benefits plan for Harbor

Shores, within a year, I stepped down[38] and headed to Buffalo, New York to lead the Buffalo Olmsted Parks Conservancy.

MORE THAN A WALK IN THE PARK

Frederick Law Olmsted is considered the father of American landscape architecture. He is probably America's most famous landscape architect, with New York City's Central Park as his most iconic design. After the creation of Central Park in the mid-nineteenth century, the good city fathers in Buffalo had invited Olmsted to the western part of New York State, saying, "We want one of those parks, too!" Olmstead's idea and vision for Buffalo was not a single park—like Central Park—but a system of what became urban parks (a pioneering concept at the time for a metropolitan recreational system). Today, the Buffalo Olmsted Parks are on the national register of historic parks, with the city itself chiefly growing up around those amazing parks.

Our organization—Buffalo Olmstead Parks Conservancy—was contracted with the City of Buffalo and Erie County to manage, raise funds for, and run the park system, which is characterized by loosely connecting boulevards (parkways) and huge decorative circles strategically located throughout the entire city. I was excited by the prospect of restoring these urban parks to create more hospitable community environments for private capital investments—and not just in the nicest parts of the city. This jewel of a park system extended to all of the major parts of Buffalo, which meant it could also extend economic value to all of parts of the city. This could begin to create conditions for private capital to not only revitalize the parks, but also to leverage

---

38 Julie Swidwa, "CWCC head steps down after one year on the job," *The Herald Pallidum,* February 22, 2006, accessed November 29, 2016, http://www.heraldpalladium.com/localnews/cwcc-head-steps-down-after-one-year-on-the-job/article_303e39f0-3cef-5a53-aac3-a7b13c1bb836.html.

these unique urban assets to stimulate other development that would exist throughout the entire system (and therefore the entire city). A twist on conventional thinking was required to make the parks both green space *and* a citywide economic opportunity by incorporating a community economic development vision to the existing park system. And that is what I set out to do during my year and a half there.[39]

DREAM DEFERRED

I left the conservancy when I had a chance at what I thought was a dream opportunity to bring together all of my background—urban green, regional economic development, major development projects, community benefits, the Innovation Economy, civil rights, education reform, and government reform—as leader of the Urban League of Greater Cleveland.

In terms of the economy, Cleveland is more of a traditional manufacturing community, redefining itself for the twenty-first century. It also is a place where "more than half of the city's kids—54 percent—live in poverty, the second highest rate of any big city nationally."[40] With one of the greatest gaps in the nation in terms of education achievement,[41]

---

39 Tracy Drury, "Holifield takes vision to parks," *Buffalo Business First*, September 18, 2006, accessed November 29, 2016, http://www.bizjournals.com/buffalo/stories/2006/09/18/story7.html.

40 Brie Zeltner, , "More than half of Cleveland kids live in poverty, and it's making them sick," September 30, 2014, accessed August 24, 2015, http://www.cleveland.com/healthfit/index.ssf/2014/09/more_than_half_of_cleveland_ki.html.

41 "Cleveland's Achievement Gap is Massive and Growing, New Index Confirms," Education Equality Index, March 23, 2016, accessed November 29, 2016, http://www.educationequalityindex.org/clevelands-achievement-gap-is-massive-and-growing-new-index-confirms/.

economic opportunities,[42] and income inequality[43] for its residents (compared to others living in nearby communities), Cleveland can be a difficult place to succeed.

To address chronic, persistent poverty and other social, education, and economic ills, Cleveland has a preponderance of singularly direct-service organizations. What I envisioned, however, was to help the Urban League provide a different kind of leadership, evolving from an organization almost singularly focused on twentieth century challenges and opportunities to one squarely focused on the twenty-first century. I wanted to help create a leadership organization focused on social, economic, and education inclusion and competitiveness, exponential impact, and meeting the needs of disconnected Clevelanders in a dramatically changed world.

One of my greatest challenges was overcoming the tyranny of tradition and narrowly purposed funding. This challenge is not unusual; nearly all organizations serving disconnected communities are hamstrung because they are virtually exclusively funded with restricted grants that generally limit what they do to what they have always done. That's because, in a restricted grant situation, the organizations are at the mercy of the funding source. So if the funding source does not like a certain idea, the grant recipients are not at liberty to explore those ideas. To this end, I address the necessity, definition, and activity of Trim Tab Organizations in Chapter 4.

Restricted grants and legacy of singularly direct services were not the Urban League's only problems: when I arrived, the new chairman

---

42   Charles Lewis, "Cleveland and Philly Rank High in Economic Inequality," *Congressional Research Institute for Social Work and Policy*, July 18, 2016, accessed November 29, 2016, http://crispinc.org/2016/07/18/cleveland-and-philly-rank-high-in-economic-inequality/.

43   Dave Davis, "Income inequality on the rise in Northeast Ohio," *The Cleveland Plain Dealer*, December 1, 2011, accessed November 29, 2016, http://blog.cleveland.com/metro/2011/12/income_inequality_on_the_rise_1.html.

and I began to meticulously go through the financial position of the organization to learn they were carrying approximately $2.7 million in accumulated debts.[44] The situation was dire; not only did they not have the funds they needed to make payments on a new building, but with all of the debt and maxed-out credit lines, they had zero capacity to pay back their other creditors. We were astounded to discover that a mere month before I took the job, a $250,000 line of credit was taken out that was supposed to be repaid in ninety days.

My entire tenure with the Urban League was spent running around the community with the chairman, trying to turn around the organization. But at the end of the day, we were not successful. The organization was unable to pay me, and it could not pay anyone else that was not directly funded by one of the restricted grants. The organization ended up going from about twenty employees to five, and as CEO, I actually presided over the elimination of my own job.[45] The organization just could not live up to the employment agreement.

The situation may have been abysmal, but it was filled with many great lessons that have informed my thoughts and actions since those days. The issues I speak about today with certitude and great conviction are informed by real experiences. These opportunities have allowed me to experience, firsthand, which approaches and methods work, why others do not, and which ones *can* work with the right organizational models, partnerships, vision, resources, and leadership.

---

44   Tom Breckenridge, "Urban League of Greater Cleveland to close its doors," *The Cleveland Plain Dealer,* May 19, 2009, accessed November 29, 2016, http://blog. cleveland.com/metro/2009/05/urban_league_of_greater_clevel.html.

45   Clara Roberts, "Urban League trims staff, eliminates CEO's job," *The Cleveland Plain Dealer,* August 4, 2009, accessed November 29, 2016, http://blog.cleveland.com/metro/2009/08/urban_league_trims_staff_elimi.html.

NEW BEGINNINGS WITH NORTECH

After the Urban League, I aggregated all my experiences to launch a consulting firm. Highlights of my practice included working with a community partner to win support from county government to develop the area's first community benefits plan, which was connected to a $425 million development project.[46] This plan ignited local interest in community benefits, resulting in new city[47] and county[48] policy to ensure benefits from large-scale construction projects broadly inure to residents. I was also retained by the leading regional land conservancy to develop the underlying rationale for a new urban-focused initiative,[49] resulting in a groundbreaking statewide institute employing land acquisition and banking strategies to assist areas decimated by home and property foreclosures.[50]

I was then retained by NorTech, Cleveland—one of Ohio's first tech-based economic development organizations and led by a visionary CEO—as the subject matter expert for one of the only assessments of the economic performance of Blacks and Hispanics in regional industry clusters. This consulting role led to the creation of a position for me:

---

46 Laura Johnston, "Cuyahoga County awards $75,000 contract to create community benefits program," *The Cleveland Plain Dealer,* May 27, 2010, updated May 28, 2010, accessed November 29, 2016, http://www.cleveland.com/cuyahoga-county/index. ssf/2010/05/cuyahoga_county_awards_75000_contract_to_create_commu-nity_benefits_program.html.

47 "Community Benefits Agreement," City of Cleveland website, accessed November 29, 2016, http://www.city.cleveland.oh.us/CityofCleveland/Home/Government/CityAgencies/OfficeofEqualOpportunity/CommunityBenefitsAgreement.

48 "Cuyahoga County Community Benefit and Opportunity Initiative," Policy Matters Ohio website, December 16, 2014, accessed November 29, 2016, http://www.policymattersohio.org/cuyahoga-community-benefit.

49 Johnathan M. Holifield, "The Case for an Urban Initiative ... The Land Conservancy Way," Western Reserve Land Conservancy, December 10, 2010, accessed November 29, 2016, http://www.leveragepointdevelopment.com/Reports/Entries/2011/3/1_2010_Reports_files/Land%20Conservancy%20Urban%20Initiative.pdf.

50 Jim Rokakis, "Thriving Communities," Western Reserve Land Conservancy, accessed November 29, 2016, http://www.wrlandconservancy.org/whatwedo/advoca-cy-and-research/.

it encapsulated my passions and was dedicated to both economic inclusion and competitiveness. I became vice president of *Inclusive Competitiveness*—perhaps the first position of its kind within an innovation-focused organization in the U.S.! NorTech's adoption of *Inclusive Competitiveness* was a major step forward.

As a leader in this organization, I became increasingly known as the "Architect of *Inclusive Competitiveness*," bridging traditional notions of economic inclusion and regional competitiveness. While at NorTech I successfully advocated for an interdisciplinary process that the Cuyahoga County Executive adopted. Reflecting my strong ethos, the process called for blending social, human, and educational services with the economic development infrastructure. The goal? To create new openings that would connect disconnected communities with the best regional economic opportunities.[51] In addition, I helped to influence local philanthropy to evolve its decade-long Innovation Economy investment strategy. Before that time, their strategy only tangentially impacted disconnected communities. The new plan however, explicitly included a unification of these populations with regional economic competitiveness priorities. These are what they now call the "growth and opportunity" and "core city" agendas. I also worked closely with leading science and entrepreneurship organizations to win a $5 million investment from the State of Ohio[52] to create the first statewide STEM education and entrepreneurship program for high school students.[53]

---

51   "Text from Cuyahoga County Executive Armond Budish's Inaugural Address," Office of the Executive, Cuyahoga County, accessed December 3, 2016, http://executive. cuyahogacounty.us/en-US/Inaugural-Address.aspx.

52   "High school entrepreneurship competition launched with $5 million in State funding," *STEM blog™, A Project of STEM Connector*, accessed November 29, 2016, http://blog. stemconnector.org/high-school-entrepreneurship-competition-launched-5-million-state-funding.

53   "Ohio Scholarship Supports Students In Math And Science," Associated Press, *WOUB Digital*, March 21, 2013, accessed November 29, 2016, http://woub.org/2013/03/21/ohio-scholarship-supports-students-math-and-science/.

FIRST-OF-ITS-KIND PROJECT IN OHIO

In 2013, I had the honor to meet and work with Dr. Patricia A. Ackerman, a regent of the Ohio Board of Regents. Now known as the Ohio Department of Higher Education (ODHE), it is a cabinet-level agency for the governor of the State of Ohio. Its role is to oversee the University System of Ohio—comprised of fourteen research universities, twenty-four regional campuses, and twenty-three community colleges.

Though a self-described "techno-weenie," when I introduced Dr. Ackerman to the concept of *Inclusive Competitiveness*, she immediately "got it." I mean she caught fire and became one of its biggest advocates!

Dr. Ackerman invited me to make the case for *Inclusive Competitiveness* during a meeting of the ODHE. Immediately following my presentation (titled "New Policy and Action to Improve the Performance of Underrepresented Ohioans in the Innovation Economy") the ODHE created the Subcommittee on *Inclusive Competitiveness*. Dr. Ackerman was asked to lead it and I was retained in a consulting capacity.

It was another breakthrough. For the first time, stewards of a state university system convened a task force to propose a statewide education and economic inclusion and competitiveness framework of actions: a comprehensive agenda which included policies, strategies, and practices that could effectively and efficiently improve the education, employment, and job-creating entrepreneurship performance of underrepresented Ohioans.

Under Dr. Ackerman's leadership, the subcommittee traveled the state, engaging thought and action leaders from government, higher education, industry and nonprofit minority, rural, philanthropic, and innovation intermediary organizations. Their primary aim was to examine the status of the above-mentioned efforts and explore ways they could be improved.

After extensive review by several layers of state government including the Governor's Office, the subcommittee's final report, *Inclusive Competitiveness: Empowering Underrepresented Ohioans to Compete in the Innovation Economy,* was unanimously adopted by the ODHE. Today, as lead drafter, I am proud to say that it serves as the nation's first strategic blueprint for building inclusive education and economic competitiveness frameworks. It could allow Ohio to become the national model. A deeper dive into the work of the ODHE is provided in Chapter 5.

FOUNDING SCALEUP PARTNERS

Today, I am a co-founder of ScaleUp Partners, the nation's leading consultancy advancing *Inclusive Competitiveness.* Along with my colleague and thought partner, Mike Green, over the past several years ScaleUp Partners has made meaningful contributions, including holding several U.S. firsts: the summit on angel investing, higher growth entrepreneurship, STEM education, and policymaking in urban communities;[54] the conference on urban and minority biomedical entrepreneurship;[55] and the summit on *Inclusive Competitiveness.*[56] Additionally, ScaleUp Partners' advocacy has spanned the country, from the White House[57] to South By

---

54 Derek T. Dingle, "Making Gangsta Moves in the Innovation Economy: Creativity, persistence, capital and connections will drive the advancement of high-growth African American businesses," *Black Enterprise Magazine,* November 22, 2011, accessed November 29, 2016, http://www.blackenterprise.com/blogs/making-gangsta-moves-in-the-innovation-economy/.

55 Catherine Podojil, "Minority biomedical entrepreneurs teach and learn at first national conference in Cleveland," *Hi Velocity Media,* May 17, 2012, accessed November 29, 2016, http://www.hivelocitymedia.com/features/minoritybiomedicalentrepreneurs031712.aspx.

56 Maria Saporta, "Clark Atlanta University leveraging concept of *inclusive competitiveness,*" *Saporta Report,* April 25, 2016, accessed November 29, 2016, http://saportareport.com/clark-atlanta-university-leveraging-concept-inclusive-competitiveness/.

57 Charlotte Young, "White House Summit Recognizes Pros And Cons Of Black Entrepreneurship *Madamenoire,* April 27, 2012, accessed December 2, 2016, http://madamenoire.com/170943/white-house-summit-recognize-pros-and-cons-of-black-entrepreneurship/.

Southwest®[58] to Silicon Valley[59] and numerous points in between. Our goal is to introduce the *Inclusive Competitiveness* narrative across the country and move it toward material action around the *IC Framework*.

LESSONS LEARNED

Although at times we've developed profound and irreconcilable differences, throughout my career I have been fortunate to work with great people. For my part, I have made groundbreaking contributions and have endured humbling professional defeats. My leadership has been celebrated and it has been maligned. I've created new executive positions, roles, and functions within market-leading organizations and have lost three executive jobs within just five years! All of these experiences, both good and difficult, have made me who I am today—a man with deep conviction for helping communities and organizations design policies, systems, and frameworks that I believe will result in sustainable places and competitive citizens.

The widespread adoption of such a comprehensive blueprint means that increasingly, citizens do not have to leave their own communities for good economic opportunities and they can successfully compete for and win top jobs. Within that vision, I am committed to helping others understand the value of *Inclusive Competitiveness*. It embodies the virtue of American exceptionalism—consistent with notions of our special character as a uniquely free nation based on democratic ideals, personal liberty, performance and productivity, and equal (and equitable)

---

58   Mike Green, "SXSWedu Launches Next Big Idea: *Inclusive Competitiveness*," *The Huffington Post,* March 4 2013, accessed November 29, 2016, http://www.huffingtonpost.com/mike-green/sxswedu-launches-next-big_b_2765038.html.

59   Mike Green, "UNCF, Stanford University Produce Historic HBCU Innovation Summit in Silicon Valley," *The Huffington Post,* December 9, 2013, accessed November 29, 2016, http://www.huffingtonpost.com/mike-green/uncf-stanford-university-_b_4408533.html.

opportunity. It can be a cornerstone for our shared economic success in the Innovation Economy.

Interestingly, *Inclusive Competitiveness* dovetails nicely with my personal contrarian nature. First, it is *disruptive.* Unfortunately, when some people hear the word "disruptive" they equate that with "destructive"; however, that is neither the intent nor the meaning of this word.

In fact, Harvard Business School Professor Clayton M. Christensen, who is the architect of and the world's foremost authority on "disruptive innovation," defines it as one that simply creates a new market and value network while displacing the established market leaders and alliances with new contributors (such as those disconnected people and communities).[60]

In the spirit of Christensen's model, *Inclusive Competitiveness* and the *IC Framework* are disruptive processes that can create new markets and opportunities where none exist and address what are perceived by innovation and investor incumbents to be less competitive assets, i.e., people, communities, and enterprises.[61]

It takes the disruptive nature of daring to challenge the status quo to create the much-needed changes. Greater economic opportunities for more people will result from a new paradigm that acknowledges that to be "inclusive" and "competitive" are not mutually exclusive exploits.

Writing this book has allowed me to communicate my beliefs and passion for economic inclusion and competitiveness with an eye to raising its profile to a national and international level. My aim is to lay down an *IC Framework* and provide the necessary steps communities must take to realize success. At the same time, the framework allows

---

60 Christensen, C., Raynor, M., McDonald, R., "What is Disruptive Innovation?" *Harvard Business Review*, December 2014, accessed November 29, 2016, https://hbr.org/2015/12/what-is-disruptive-innovation.

61 Ibid.

the freedom and power for the communities themselves to decide how best to navigate their own journey by applying the framework to their unique community, population, challenges, needs, and opportunities.

I believe that now is the perfect time for communities to embrace this new economic paradigm, as interest in the Innovation Economy has grown. Moreover, it is time for people to initiate new conversations about the economy, their communities, and what is needed now to make a positive difference in their quality of life. And it is not just for their own interests but for those of the entire community and for future generations as well.

The chief lesson I have learned can be wonderfully summed up this way: the secret of change is to focus all of your energy not on fighting the old, but on building the new.[62] *Inclusive Competitiveness* is about building the new.

MY UVP

Businesses try to differentiate their products and services from the competition by highlighting a UVP, or unique value proposition. Maybe their UVP will aim to communicate that their appliance is better, or less expensive, or that their service delivers more quality or more value than that of other companies.

I have thought a lot about my personal UVP—or what differentiates me from others who are concerned about our economy and its future. In that process, I have come to realize that the entirety of my life's experiences have crystallized into a single intention: to prosecute a War for Opportunity. We each have a contribution to make and I am an opportunity warrior. My uncommon history and background—as a

---

62 Dan Millman, *Way of the Peaceful Warrior: A Book That Changes Lives*, HJ Kramer, Tiburon, CA - New World Library, Novato, CA; 20th Anniversary edition, September 30, 2000, 105.

NAACP civil rights lawyer/advocate, community development champion, education and government reformer, and "big time" regional technology- and innovation-based economic developer—have created my life's focus. The unique blend of my experiences has put me in good stead to pursue my passion and lend a distinctive voice and perspective on the issues I believe really matter in our collective economic future.

I sincerely believe that the opportunities that I have been afforded are extremely rare. They have conspired to make me who I am and allow me the privilege to do the work that I do. I am intensely mindful that I manage to make a difference. Over the course of my career, my beliefs have refined and sharpened. I would like to think that I have grown personally and that I am more coachable, open, and approachable now than I've ever been.

In the words of James Taylor: "That's why I'm here." I am here to reflect and build upon the positive aspects of disconnected people and communities. I am here to help them to view themselves through a new lens. I am here to help them adopt new dreams—not only to survive but also to harness the full power of the Innovation Economy. So please join me in the next chapter for a revealing look at the quest for and legacy weaknesses of the U.S.' pursuit of global economic competitiveness and how it can (and must) evolve toward *Inclusive Competitiveness.*

CHAPTER 3

ECONOMIC COMPETITIVENESS 2.0

INTRODUCING INCLUSIVE COMPETITIVENESS

"Those Damn Computers" and

Economic Competitiveness

The situation comedy show *Good Times* was a must-see in our home, as it was for many Americans during the 1970s. One episode, titled "J.J. Becomes a Man," aired in two parts in September 1974. It detailed the arrest of J.J. on his birthday for suspicion of holding up a liquor store. Other than serving as entertainment for a then ten-year-old child, nothing about it struck me as remarkable—until I saw the episode again in the year 2000. It was then I realized that the Evans family of 1974 was relevant to today's Innovation Economy.

In the year 2000, I pioneered, along with business and education leaders and innovation advocates, the effort to establish Greater Cincinnati's first regional technology and innovation leadership council.[63] My outlook was now decidedly different. I now viewed the story from the perspective of a regional technology and innovation development *leader* rather than an elementary school spectator. It gave me new insight into the social and economic dimensions of the Evans family's predicament and the potential far-reaching implications.

To summarize the episode: J.J.'s father, James, is unable to obtain credit from a local department store to buy his son a special eighteenth birthday gift. Returning home angry with the disappointing news he said something like this: "It used to be that a man's word meant something. Now it's *those damn computers.*"

"Hmmm," I thought, "*Those damn computers.*"

The episode unfolded with J.J., who had just scored a new job, being falsely arrested. While J.J. was still in jail, the family sent his sister, Thelma, to inform his new employer that he could not report for work on his first day. Thelma gave a phony excuse for J.J.'s absence.

Fast forward: J.J. is released from jail, and the family is celebrating his freedom when Thelma arrives on the scene with bad news—J.J. has lost his job because of the arrest. The family is crushed and asks: "How could they know about the arrest so fast?"

James, who is now furious, answers: "I know how they knew—it's *those damn computers.*"

Reflecting later on what I had seen, I began to wonder how much of the exclamation, "*those damn computers,*" a sentiment that connotes

---

63   Rachel Melcer, "Chamber leader wants bigger tech tent: Johnathan Holifield, tapped to build a regional technology council, hopes to organize and unite the city's disparate job-attraction efforts," *Cincinnati Business Courier*, May 22, 2000, accessed November 29, 2016, http://www.bizjournals.com/cincinnati/stories/2000/05/22/story6.html.

suspicion of technology and innovation, has informed the economic narrative, ideas, and beliefs of Blacks and other citizens largely disconnected from the Innovation Economy. Perhaps those early sentiments and messages—delivered and received at the dawn of the computer and technology revolution—were adversely affecting how disconnected Americans even today think about economic competitiveness and the opportunities, empowerment, and the prosperity that attaches to it.

That short, repeated phrase in a television show is simply representative of the suspicion and reticence of so many people to move into this technological revolution and not just be taken along for the ride. I look around today and still see many engaging new technology and innovation as consumers, but too few who are preparing to engage them as producers. Some of this may be traced back to the kinds of utterances on shows like *Good Times*. There is still a large segment of our population who remains unaware or, even worse, unreasonably suspicious about technology. They take advantage of so many of the conveniences of their day-to-day devices without embracing and seeing technology and innovation development as a way to economically advance and prosper. By and large those communities tend to be disconnected demographically and geographically from new opportunities in multiple ways, shapes, and forms.

REDEFINING ECONOMIC COMPETITIVENESS

For at least the past thirty years, as a federal policy priority, the U.S. has fixated on global economic competition. One of the challenges faced by early proponents of U.S. economic competitiveness "was to define

[it] because many Americans didn't believe there was a problem."[64] For most, since World War II, U.S. global economic leadership was unquestioned. Today, generally we understand that other nations have closed important economic gaps and that our economic supremacy is no longer a foregone conclusion.

Despite Americans' growing appreciation of the challenges of competing in the global economy, use of term "competitiveness" has been largely reserved for government, business, academic, and economic leaders. It has not found its way to common usage among ordinary citizens. The absence of this term in regular social, education, and economic discourse is the beginning of community misalignment with, and disconnection from, the best opportunities our cities, regions, states, and nation have to offer—and is the driving imperative for this book.

Traditionally, economic competitiveness has focused on national productivity driven by businesses' success. For example, The World Economic Forum has defined economic competitiveness "as the set of institutions, policies, and factors that determine the level of productivity of a country."[65] This singular focus on business and national productivity has proved insufficient; the U.S. has shown extraordinary and steady growth in productivity over the decades, yet there has not been a proportionate increase in economic prosperity commensurate with that growth.

Michael Porter, Jan Rivkin, and their colleagues at Harvard Business School have taken a new look at national economic competitiveness, boldly redefining what it means for the U.S. to have a competitive

---

64 Max Holland, "Mr. Young Goes to Washington," *Washington Decoded,* December 5, 1999, accessed November 29, 2016, http://www.washingtondecoded.com/site/1999/12/mr-young-goes-t.html.
65 "The Global Competitiveness Report 2014-2015," The World Economic Forum: http://www.weforum.org/reports/global-competitiveness-report-2014-2015.

economy.[66] They define "U.S. competitiveness as the ability of firms in the U.S. to succeed in the global marketplace *while raising the living standards of the average American* [emphasis added]."[67]

This is a superior definition of U.S. economic competitiveness because in order for our economy to succeed we need companies to start and grow here, want to locate here, and/or operate profitably here.[68] At the same time, an economy is not successful if most of the people in it are experiencing a stagnant or declining standard of living. Both kinds of success are important, and each depends, in part, on the other.[69]

Moreover, the Harvard Business School approach to measuring national economic competitiveness spans the partisan divide.[70] Conservatives usually focus on how well corporations are doing, and progressives usually focus on living standards and how income is distributed.[71]

In my experience, a perceptual problem exists: much of what passes for economic competitiveness in cities, regions, and states is actually narrowly focused business competitiveness. Business competitiveness is absolutely a necessary piece of economic competitiveness. On its own however, it is insufficient for the desired improvements in both national economic performance and quality of life—particularly for disconnected Americans.

---

66   David Brodwin, "A New Look at U.S. Economic Competitiveness: The U.S. economy has failed to create many jobs in the big, strategically important, globally competitive industries," *U.S. News & World Report*, September 4, 2012, accessed November 29, 2016, http://www.usnews.com/opinion/blogs/economic-intelligence/2012/09/04/a-new-look-at-us-economic-competitiveness.
67   Ibid.
68   Ibid.
69   Ibid.
70   Ibid.
71   Ibid.

EMPLOYMENT "AND" ENTREPRENEURSHIP

With the evolution away from the agrarian to the industrial economy, wage labor[72] became the leading form of employment in the U.S. Along with industrialization came the expectation for people to be gainfully employed or "get a good job." More than ever, during the second half of the twentieth century to this day, families, friends, teachers, counselors, and others have broadened that expectation to "get a good education and training to get a good job." These "good jobs" can be defined as more traditional positions that:

- Are in the upper third by median wages of occupations in which they are classified,
- Earn about $53,000 annually for a full-time, full-year worker, and
- Incorporate a variety of other factors, such as job satisfaction, access to benefits, job security, working conditions, and job meaningfulness.[73]

Concentrating on education and training only to secure gainful employment is not sufficient to build an inclusive, prosperous future for our nation. Disconnected Americans must also pursue and acquire the skills needed to *create* new jobs. In the twenty-first century, there is need to articulate and inculcate in disconnected communities the dual and complementary expectations to leverage their education and training to both attain top employment opportunities and become the

---

72 "Wage-labour," Encyclopedia.com, accessed November 29, 2016, http://www. encyclopedia.com/doc/1O88-wagelabour.html.

73 Anthony P. Carnevale, Tamara Jayasundera and Artem Gulish ,"GOOD JOBS ARE BACK: College Graduates Are First in Line 2015," McCourt School of Public Policy at Georgetown University, April 27, 2014, accessed November 29, 2016, https://cew. georgetown.edu/wp-content/uploads/Good-Jobs_Full_Final.pdf.

higher growth entrepreneurs who create not only their own job, but perhaps jobs for other Americans.

UNPRECEDENTED CHALLENGES: INNOVATION ECONOMY SQUEEZE[74]

America is confronting twin forces that challenge us in new and profound ways. It is called the Innovation Economy Squeeze: we live in an increasingly "flat world"[75] where competition for jobs stretches to nearly every corner of the globe. It is compounded by the dramatic gains in technology-driven efficiency, with as many as 47 percent of U.S. jobs at risk for automation over the forthcoming decades.[76] This efficiency has been a double-edged sword. While we have seen a massive increase in U.S. business productivity, it has been accompanied by a decline in the creation of traditional good jobs.

Billions of people—new economic competitors—now have access to improved commercial opportunities in the global economy. Within the current paradigm, clearly all people around the world do not have completely equitable opportunity and employment. However, the flatter economic landscape does make it more accessible for more people to compete for jobs and opportunity than ever before.

The decoupling of business productivity increases from traditional good job creation is a phenomenon clearly evidenced in the U.S. manufacturing sector—a familiar friend and entry point for disconnected

---

74   Johnathan M. Holifield, Refers to the increasing pressure on workers due to business efficiency gains from new technology and automation and global competition for jobs, 2010.

75   Thomas L. Friedman, "The World is Flat: A Brief History of the Twenty-first Century," Farar, Straus and Giroux, New York, NY, updated and expanded edition, 2007, p. x.

76   Carl Benedikt Frey and Michael A. Osborne, "The Future of Employment: How Susceptible are Jobs to Computerisation?" September 17, 2013, accessed September 1, 2016, http://www.oxfordmartin.ox.ac.uk/downloads/academic/The_Future_of_Employment.pdf.

Americans into the middle class. For example, in 1953 manufacturing accounted for 28 percent of U.S. GDP, according to the U.S. Bureau of Economic Analysis.[77] By 1980 that had dropped to 20 percent, and it reached 12 percent in 2012. Over that time, U.S. GDP increased from $2.6 trillion to $15.5 trillion, which means that absolute manufacturing output grew exponentially over sixty years. Those goods were produced by fewer people.

According to the Bureau of Labor Statistics, the number of employees in manufacturing was sixteen million in 1953, nineteen million in 1980, and twelve million in 2012. Proportionally, the decline is significant: from one third, to one fifth, then to approximately one tenth of the total number of nonfarm jobs, respectively.[78]

Consequently, over the last sixty years, U.S. manufacturing productivity grew 600 percent,[79] yet these nonfarm jobs dropped from more than 30 percent to about 10 percent. Stunningly, in 1950 it required 1,000 workers to produce what 170 workers can today![80] Today's advanced manufacturing is surely a boost to the U.S. However, it will not provide good jobs at the historic levels of traditional manufacturing.

This productivity/job creation relationship leads to a threshold question: From where will America's new jobs come if more Americans are not creating them?

The Innovation Economy Squeeze is a considerable driver of the new job creation imperative.

---

77 Charles Kenny, "Factory Jobs Are Gone. Get Over It," *Bloomberg Business, Global Economics,* January 23, 2014, accessed November 29, 2016, http://www.bloomberg.com/bw/articles/2014-01-23/manufacturing-jobs-may-not-be-cure-for-unemployment-inequality.
78 Ibid.
79 William A. Strauss, Senior Economist and Economic Advisor, Federal Reserve Bank of Chicago, "Assessing Manufacturing: Output and Labor, Making It In America—Manufacturing Matters," 2012 NABE Industry Conference Cleveland, OH, May 31, 2012, accessed November 29, 2016, file:///C:/Users/jmholifield/Downloads/05-31-assessing-manufacturing-pdf%20(3).pdf.
80 Ibid.

Americans are being economically squeezed in unprecedented ways. Fewer workers are now needed to produce ever more goods and services, and billions of new workers around the world are now competing with the U.S. for new jobs. This squeeze is disproportionately felt by disconnected Americans.

INNOVATION FOR BOTH EFFICIENCY AND EXPANSION

Innovation for Efficiency. As discussed above, the Innovation Economy Squeeze is an outcome of the introduction of new innovations and technologies that have disrupted business models, given birth to new industries, and accelerated obsolescence of mature companies. It has evolved the twenty-first century marketplace to where substantially fewer workers produce ever more goods and services. The efficiency gains are a combination of the simultaneous reduction of company expenses and increases in productivity. These gains are vital for U.S. businesses to remain globally competitive but do result in lower levels of good job creation. "Innovation for efficiency" is an inescapable reality of the Innovation Economy. In effect it is a frontal assault on the new definition of U.S. economic competitiveness. As such, it is of particular concern for disconnected Americans, who tend to fare even more poorly in scenarios of lower creation of so-called good jobs.

Innovation for Expansion: The decreased reliance on human labor can be effectively addressed through innovations that create both needed business efficiency *and* expansion. To stimulate good job creation, innovation is needed within existing businesses and industries and that sparks entrepreneurship within new and emerging industries. It is essential for disconnected Americans to contribute the kind of innovations that achieve both necessary ends.

ECONOMIC INCLUSION AND COMPETITIVENESS IMPERATIVE

During the last century, America's position as the global economic leader was unaffected by lower contributions of disconnected Americans in key performance areas. We were largely the unchallenged global leaders and U.S. economic competitiveness was assured even without optimal productivity from more than half our population. This is no longer the case. With unyielding global competition for jobs and opportunity, our nation cannot continue maintaining the walls that separate too many Americans from opportunities to successfully compete and prosper. Without an economy open to more contributions from more Americans (especially disconnected populations) we accept spectacular success for a few at the expense of a resilient, globally competitive national economy that will support shared prosperity.

THE INCLUSIVE COMPETITIVENESS SOLUTION

Inclusive Competitiveness is a comprehensive response to the Innovation Economy Squeeze and our need for more Americans to contribute new innovations for business efficiency and expansion. It is an interdisciplinary framework of policies, strategies, practices, and metrics that creates community systems to improve the productivity and quality of life of disconnected Americans in the Innovation Economy. Just as importantly, it also spans the partisan divide by embracing the familiar focal points of both conservatives on business performance and progressives on standard of living and income access.

THE IC FRAMEWORK

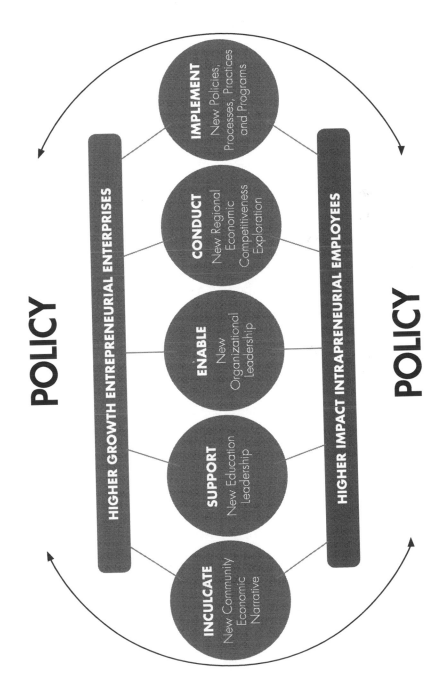

POLICY

POLICY

HIGHER GROWTH ENTREPRENEURIAL ENTERPRISES

HIGHER IMPACT INTRAPRENEURIAL EMPLOYEES

IMPLEMENT
New Policies, Processes, Practices and Programs

CONDUCT
New Regional Economic Competitiveness Exploration

ENABLE
New Organizational Leadership

SUPPORT
New Education Leadership

INCULCATE
New Community Economic Narrative

As illustrated on the previous page, the *IC Framework* is needed to achieve the ends of sustaining and improving U.S. economic competitiveness. Disconnected Americans need to develop new, interdisciplinary capacities and capabilities that create new and economically competitive proficiencies among their populations and within their communities.

Recall the beginning days of the Internet—the early-to-mid-1990s. This new and extraordinary tool greeted us all as new users with a rather static online experience. This was the age of brochureware. Typically, organizations deployed the Internet on top of their customary business practices, doing little more than transferring their printed brochures to websites or pages with little or no foresight as to the possibilities of the new medium.[81] Copy and visuals were generally inert and the online experience was mostly uninteresting and not interactive. These were perfunctory, stale encounters.

Over the course of a generation, the process has steadily reversed, with the Internet now at the bottom of what businesses, organizations, and individuals do in the marketplace. In other words, today these groups build on top of the Internet instead of their traditional practices. This turnaround is the result of a growing understanding of the power and possibilities of this vibrant mass medium. The result for users is dramatically improved and more dynamic, informative, and entertaining online experiences, such as blogs, social networking, instant messaging, interactivity, streaming media, and many others. There is really no resemblance between the early and present Internet.

This analogy holds important lessons for *Inclusive Competitiveness*. Similar to yesterday's Internet users, disconnected communities experience at best a stagnant, and at worse a nonexistent, relationship to today's local, regional, state, and national economic competitiveness

---

81   TechTarget, SearchSOA, accessed November 29, 2016, http://searchsoa.techtarget. com/definition/brochureware.

efforts. Stewards of America's Innovation Economy, and accompanying innovation and entrepreneurship ecosystems, are only beginning to understand the tremendous possibilities inherent in improving the productivity of disconnected populations. Similar to the about-face with the Internet, the *IC Framework* is designed to flip the script for the disconnected. Its goal is to drive economic inclusion and competitiveness from its present position as an afterthought (resting undisturbed atop the Innovation Economy) to an energetic, exciting, enabling role embedded at the foundation. In its evolved position it will create considerably improved economic and quality of life outcomes for disconnected Americans.

Here is the framework:

INTERDISCIPLINARY

An important distinction of *Inclusive Competitiveness* is that it is interdisciplinary. The framework is designed to engage the customary sources of local, regional, state, and national Innovation Economy leadership. This includes tech- and innovation-based economic development intermediary organizations, venture development organizations, business accelerators and incubators, and the like. But it goes a step further by also promoting new, non-traditional engagement with the social, human, and education services organizations that are prevalent in disconnected communities. This interdependence can help grow a larger and more diverse talent base of disconnected Americans to create businesses and fill jobs that expand the nation's economic competitiveness. Success is reliant upon Innovation Economy incumbents collaborating with non-traditional organizations and leaders who interact daily with millions of disconnected Americans.

ENABLING POLICY

As illustrated in the model *IC Framework*, policy is the enabling force of *Inclusive Competitiveness* that creates its requisite conditions.

The *IC Framework* definition of policy not only includes government but embraces a much larger set of organizations and interests, including private sector leadership and community groups. These multiple sources can exert significant influence on local, state, and national Innovation Economy narratives, strategies, and practices, whether through the exploration, selection, and promotion of priorities, or the funding of specific initiatives. It is important to include the influential actors who tend to elude traditional public sector channels by encompassing both the public and private sectors within the broad definition of policy.

SPECIAL ROLE FOR HGEs

Embedded in the *IC Framework* is an extremely powerful way to create more jobs–HGEs (high-growth enterprises). The political mantra that "small businesses are the nation's job creator" is only partially correct. In fact, most small businesses do not create many new jobs. Instead, it's a *certain kind* of small business that creates those new jobs. These are the young, innovative, explosive growth companies. They create a disproportionately high amount of the jobs for our nation. Oftentimes they are STEM-related: from the science, technology, engineering, and mathematics disciplines.

Higher growth entrepreneurs are motivated to create and grow HGEs as fast and as large as possible. These people are capable of producing growth companies that significantly impact regional, national, and even global economies. They are passionate about their product or service and want it to succeed dramatically in the marketplace. Higher growth entrepreneurs also want to build the largest and most valuable firm possible. In doing so they create an attractive candidate for going public, or for merger or acquisition, which are common strategies for securing additional funding to fuel rapid growth and new job creation.

It's a little-known fact that nearly all net job creation since 1980 has occurred in firms less than five years old.[82] Even less known is that HGEs "account for a disproportionate share of job creation.... In any given year, the top-performing 1 percent of companies generate roughly 40 percent of new job creation ... [and] the top 5 percent of companies (measured by employment growth), or about 273,000 firms, creates two-thirds of any new jobs in any given year." [83] In sum, the majority of job creation stems from typically young, entrepreneurial growth companies—the HGEs.

You might be asking yourself what role are the huge corporations playing. Don't they hire lots of workers? Yes, large conglomerates hire the most ... and they also fire the most, creating close to a zero-sum game. So, the real action is found within these HGEs—those fast-growing, sustainable businesses that create many new jobs.

Since the early 1990s, economic development leaders have conclusively determined that an increase in the number of entrepreneurs, particularly higher growth entrepreneurs, leads to increased job growth and economic dynamism.[84] This effect is a result of the indisputable

82   Dane Stangler and Robert E. Litan, "Where Will The Jobs Come From?" *Ewing Marion Kauffman Foundation Research Series: Firm Formation and Economic Growth*, November 2009, 2, accessed November 29, 2016, http://www.kauffman.org/~/media/kauffman_org/research%20reports%20and%20covers/2009/11/where_will_the_jobs_come_from.pdf.

83   Dane Stangler, "High-Growth Firms and the Future of the American Economy," *Ewing Marion Kauffman Foundation Research Series: Firm Formation and Economic Growth*, March 2010, 5, accessed August 8, 2015, http://www.kauffman.org/~/media/kauffman_org/research%20reports%20and%20covers/2010/04/high-growthfirmsstudy.pdf.

84   "The Importance of Young Firms for Economic Growth," An Educational Policy Brief From the Ewing Marion Kauffman Foundation, September 25, 2014, updated September 14, 2015, http://www.kauffman.org/~/media/kauffman_org/resources/2014/entrepreneurship%20policy%20digest/september%202014/entrepreneurship_policy_digest_september2014.pdf.

positive relationship between economic growth and collectively the entrepreneurs' concrete expression of their skills. Their propensity to innovate manifests as new enterprises and job creation.

By introducing new ideas, new processes, new products and services, new technologies, and new jobs, innovative higher growth entrepreneurs affect (and ultimately renew) myriad economic activities. Not only are the general economic activities of the businesses and industries of these entrepreneurs renewed, but also those of the geographic area in which the entrepreneurs are situated. New Orleans is an emerging example of economic revitalization due to the contribution of entrepreneurs in the aftermath of Hurricane Katrina.[85]

Those who create, lead, and steward regional innovation and entrepreneurship ecosystems understand the importance of HGEs: they know that to create new jobs and wealth, there needs to be more of these vital firms. Meanwhile, the disconnected populations tend to focus on small businesses, which in and of themselves are necessary. Small businesses *do* have an important role to play in any economy. However, it's not possible to generate explosive job growth by focusing solely on small businesses. That's because this genre of business is predominantly typified by "lifestyle" ventures such as restaurants, barber shops, and other small retail outlets and service providers.

It's time that we bring this distinction to light in the disconnected communities across our country. In deference to Victor Hugo, including disconnected Americans in our national thrust to create more HGEs is "an idea whose time has come."

---

85   Hakeem Hopper-Collins, "The Comeback City—How Entrepreneurs Are Helping To Revitalize New Orleans 10 Years After Hurricane Katrina," *Lioness Magazine,* March 12, 2015, accessed November 29, 2016, http://lionessmagazine.com/the-come-back-city-how-entrepreneurs-are-helping-to-revitalize-new-orleans-10-years-af-ter-hurricane-katrina/.

PRIVATE CAPITAL: MOTHER'S MILK OF HGEs

Interconnected with HGEs is the critical role of private capital. Business owners can finance their enterprises principally in two ways: debt and equity. "Debt" involves borrowing money to be repaid, plus interest, while "equity" involves raising money by selling interests in the company. Private equity is capital that is not noted on a public exchange, is composed of funds and investors that directly invest in private companies, or that engage in buyouts of public companies, making them private.[86]

Private equity capital includes angel investors[87] and venture capital.[88] It is an essential ingredient and significant lever of American innovation and economic competitiveness.

Disconnected Americans have historically financed their business enterprises with debt capital or bank loans. Typically, debt capital is difficult to access in disconnected communities, and private forms of capital are largely nonexistent. Job- and wealth-creating opportunities are therefore hampered by the inability to:

- Regularly start businesses that would be attractive to private capital investors, and
- Attract private funding even when businesses have all the hallmarks of good investment prospects for these financiers.

---

86 "What is Private Equity," Investopedia, accessed November 29, 2016, http://www.investopedia.com/terms/p/privateequity.asp.

87 Angel investors invest in small startups or entrepreneurs. Often, angel investors are among an entrepreneur's family and friends. The capital angel investors provide may be a one-time investment to help the business propel or an ongoing injection of money to support and carry the company through its difficult early stages. Investopedia, http://www.investopedia.com/terms/a/angelinvestor.asp.

88 Venture capital is financing that investors provide to startup companies and small businesses that are believed to have long-term growth potential. For startups without access to capital markets, venture capital is an essential source of money. Risk is typically high for investors, but the downside for the startup is that these venture capitalists usually get a say in company decisions. Investopedia, http://www.investopedia.com/terms/v/venturecapital.asp#ixzz4JJm4bTZ1.

The willingness of private investors to take risks in funding higher growth entrepreneurs, disruptive technologies, and new business models is responsible for creating entire new industries that today employ millions in high-paying jobs.[89] Angel and venture capital usually involves a substantial level of risk. It predicates its involvement on the growth potential of the business model and the experience, ability, vision, and passion of the business founders and owners. Also, the involvement of good private capital investors in these companies not only includes the provision of money, but other assets such as connecting entrepreneurs with customers, resources to build their teams, and opportunities for follow-on investment. Disconnected communities are isolated from comprehensive innovation and entrepreneurship ecosystems and infrastructure (at all levels, from local to national). This makes competitive venture development more difficult and therefore much less attractive to this source of funds.

Angel and venture capital activity have a particularly significant impact on the U.S. economy:

- It is a catalyst for job creation and innovation.
- It creates increased tax revenues and enhances national competitiveness.
- It fuels higher growth entrepreneurs and HGEs.

All these elements result in substantial new jobs and wealth.

As of December 2013, a review of public companies by the Stanford Graduate School of Business listed 4,063 firms with total market capitalization of $21.3 trillion. Of those, 710, or 18 percent, are venture

---

89 "Venture Impact EDITION 6.0: The Economic Importance of Venture Capital-Backed Companies to the U.S. Economy," National Venture Capital Association and IHS Global Insight, 2011, http://www.jumpstartnetwork.org/sitecore/content/jumpstartinc/home/results/dl/~/media/JumpStartInc/Images/Results-Page/2011-NVCA-Venture ImpactReport.ashx.

capital-backed.[90] Their market capitalization is $4.3 trillion (20 percent of total market capitalization) and they also employ four million people.[91] Additionally, angel capital investors are increasingly important, funding more than sixteen times as many companies as venture capitalists[92] and having surpassed them as a funding source for startup enterprises in the U.S. They are estimated to have had $24.1 billion of capital deployed in 2014, up from $17.6 billion in 2009.[93]

Thousands of companies would not exist today if it were not for the early angel and later stage venture capital investment support they received.[94] Companies such as Federal Express, Staples, The Home Depot, Outback Steakhouse, and Starbucks are well-known examples of "traditional" companies that were launched with angel[95] and venture capital.[96] Technology companies such as Cisco, Google, eBay, Yahoo, and many others were all, at one time, just ideas that needed the startup funds and guidance that these forms of private capital provide.[97]

To embrace this twenty-first century economic prosperity tool, disconnected Americans have to become more aware of the important

90   Ilya A. Strebulaev and Will Gornall, "How Much Does Venture Capital Drive the U.S. Economy?
Two scholars measure the economic impact of VC-funded companies," Stanford Graduate School of Business, October 21, 2015, accessed November 29, 2016, https://www.gsb.stanford.edu/insights/how-much-does-venture-capital-drive-us-economy.

91   Ibid.

92   Diane Mulcahy, "Six Myths About Venture Capitalists," *Harvard Business Review,* May 2013, accessed November 29, 2016, https://hbr.org/2013/05/six-myths-about-venture-capitalists.

93   Laurent Belsie,"How Angel Investors Help Startup Firms," The National Bureau of Economic Research, accessed September 4, 2016, http://www.nber.org/digest/mar16/w21808.html.

94   "Testimony of Sherrill Neff," Quaker BioVentures, for the Joint Economic Committee of Congress, July 10, 2008, accessed November 30, 2016, http://www.jec.senate.gov/public/_cache/files/37a4b193-6355-4c78-a30d-109f47fe841d/neffjecpensionhearing071008.pdf.

95   Marianne Hudson, "ACA, Angel Groups, and Angel-Backed Companies," Angel Capital Association, September, 2012, accessed November 30, 2016, http://www.angelcapitalassociation.org/data/Documents/Resources/ACAandAngelGroupBackground09-12.pdf.

96   "Testimony of Sherrill Neff," Quaker BioVentures.

97   Ibid.

role angel and venture capital play in our economy. The *IC Framework* welcomes and supports private capital in all its forms. Not as a single silver bullet for financing new businesses, but as part of the "silver buckshot" that comprises *Inclusive Competitiveness.*

Below are the interconnected ways that we can move forward.

STRATEGY ELEMENTS

- **Instill New Community Economic Narrative:** Narratives refer to the leading economic culture, leadership, and advocacy in disconnected communities. They inform the kinds of education, employment, and entrepreneurship support services and opportunities that are demanded by and available in these communities. They are not easily measurable factors. Self-described "social ecologist," who was hailed as "the man who invented management," Peter Drucker, famously said "Culture eats strategy for breakfast."[98] In other words, for a strategy to prevail it must be aligned with and supported by overall cultural objectives. New economic narratives that manifest as new economic culture are the foundations of *Inclusive Competitiveness.* The patent absence of twenty-first century economic narratives in disconnected communities impedes productivity in the Innovation Economy. New narratives among the disconnected are needed that connect to and support the nation's leading economic competitiveness thrusts. Because they are intangible and complex in nature, we generally do not accord narratives the importance they deserve. There is massive untapped potential that resides in disconnected communities that is at great risk of remaining on the sidelines. The time for an evolution of community economic narratives is

---

98 "Peter Drucker's Life and Legacy," Drucker Institute, accessed November 29, 2016, http://www.druckerinstitute.com/peter-druckers-life-and-legacy/.

now. One that focuses on the Innovation Economy imperatives and puts a high priority on education, particularly STEM/STEAM (science, technology, engineering, art, math), higher impact employment, and higher growth entrepreneurship.

- **Support New Education Leadership:** Improving the country's economic competitiveness is inextricably linked to high proficiency and expertise in the STEM and STEAM disciplines. STEM is already a national education priority. The follow-on effects of lower STEM education attainment of disconnected Americans are significant. It reflects in lower productivity in the Innovation Economy. New leadership from K-12 through higher education institutions is needed to fill or perhaps even flood the pipeline of disconnected high school and college students toward STEM disciplines. These students can become our new economic athletes. Engaging disconnected communities in meaningful discourse on the importance of STEM education to win the best jobs and create high-performing companies is critical for driving economic competitiveness and prosperity. STEM education achievement gaps today will result in staggering job and wealth disparities tomorrow. Importantly, these new efforts must be balanced by a strong co-focus on entrepreneurship. This dual, educational thrust—education both to get and create jobs—is at the heart of *Inclusive Competitiveness.*

Embracing STEAM: Over the past decade, women's share of undergraduate degrees has steadily increased, representing about 57 percent of bachelor's degrees awarded by U.S. institutions in 2012.[99] However, the share of women earning STEM degrees has not increased, holding remarkably steady at about 37 percent.[100] Moreover, the number of Blacks earning bachelor's degrees increased by an impressive 41 percent,[101] and the number of Hispanics earning undergraduate degrees increased by an extraordinary 85 percent in the last dozen or so years.[102] However, when it comes to STEM, these groups are lagging far behind their peers. By age twenty-four, Blacks will comprise only 2.7 percent and Hispanics just 2.2 percent of the U.S. STEM graduate population.[103]

In real terms these groups represent a huge quantity of non-STEM or potential STEM-talent currently confined to the sidelines watching the game instead of contributing. With today's relentless worldwide competition for jobs and opportunity, sustaining our nation's global economic leadership requires greater contributions from many more Americans—including these groups.

Without distracting from worthy efforts to improve STEM education attainment of women, Blacks, and Hispanics, STEAM provides a complementary means to identify, capture, and

---

99 Margaret E. Blume-Kohout, "Understanding the Gender Gap In STEM Fields Entrepreneurship for the U.S. Small Business Administration," October 2014, accessed November 29, 2016, https://www.sba.gov/sites/default/files/Gender%20Gap%20in%20STEM%20Fields_0.pdf.
100 Ibid.
101 Laura Merner, "African American Participation among Bachelors in the Physical Sciences and Engineering," American Institute of Physics, November 15, 2015, accessed November 29, 2016, https://www.aip.org/sites/default/files/statistics/minorities/africanamer-pse-13.1.pdf.
102 Laura Merner, "Report: More Hispanics Earning Bachelor's Degrees in Physical Sciences and Engineering," American Institute of Physics, December 3, 2014, accessed November 29, 2016, https://www.aip.org/news/2014/report-more-hispanics-earning-bachelor%E2%80%99s-degrees-physical-sciences-and-engineering.
103 Jeffrey Mervis, "New Answers for Increasing Minorities in Science," Science Magazine, September 30, 2010, accessed November 29, 2016, http://www.sciencemag.org/news/2010/09/new-answers-increasing-minorities-science.

connect the growing cache of non-STEM talent and creativity to top employment opportunities, as well as higher growth entrepreneurship.

- **Promote New Organizational Leadership:** Disconnected Americans are served by a rich and diverse set of leadership organizations that typically provide direct and place-based services to residents. Their focus is on areas such as traditional community economic development and education, employment, human, small business, and social services. New organizational leadership is required to inject incumbent services with new strategies, capacities, and capabilities that are aligned with local, state, and U.S. economic competitiveness levers/opportunities. New organizational leadership that builds new bridges to this twenty-first century infrastructure, on which the nation is counting to deliver future jobs and wealth, is required to achieve *Inclusive Competitiveness* outcomes.

- **Conduct New Regional Economic Competitiveness Exploration, Selection, and Prioritization.** An appropriate emphasis on *Inclusive Competitiveness* is needed in the early stages of strategic planning for economic competitiveness, including the exploration, selection, and prioritization of Innovation Economy areas of focus, programs, and initiatives in cities, regions, and states throughout the U.S. Without such emphasis on the front-end, the *Inclusive Competitiveness* challenges associated with the chosen strategies can become nearly insurmountable during back-end implementation. Importantly, the full set of an area's Innovation Economy priorities cannot be limited to only those economic sectors that create job opportunities for the most highly educated workers in a city or region or the nation. New and complementary approaches are needed to promote widespread growth and development, especially in disconnected communities. New activity that is typically associated with good jobs, with lower barriers to entry, is needed to create opportunities that include accessible education and training for workers and accessible technical assistance and capital for would-be entrepreneurs.

- **Adopt New Policies, Processes, and Practices:** The opposite of risk-averse is to be risk-astute. Creative, risk-astute policy, process, and practice advancements across a diverse set of policymaking stakeholders—who substantially underwrite the nation's economic competitiveness activities—are required to activate and sustain *Inclusive Competitiveness*. These stakeholders include business, community, technology, and innovation economic development organizations, disconnected-serving organizations, colleges and universities, and government and philanthropic institutions. As explained in this chapter, the existing economic narratives and education attainment levels in disconnected communities make forming new job-creating enterprises difficult. The situation is exacerbated in these areas by the absence of innovation and entrepreneurship ecosystem development. The cycle must be broken with new risk-astute assessments of and investments in Innovation Economy opportunities in disconnected communities. To achieve greatly, overcoming the current low risk/low reward climate, there must be higher risk tolerance among the policymaking stakeholders that support U.S. economic competitiveness, as well as invest in disconnected communities. It's time to blend these heretofore separate thrusts, innovating incumbent strategies with new, interdisciplinary approaches that can yield specific findings, scalable solutions, and replicable ways to improve the economic competitiveness of these Americans.

DESIRED OUTCOMES

Inclusive Competitiveness builds dual pipelines of improved performance and productivity by preparing higher impact intrapreneurs (employees infused with the ethic of entrepreneurship) as well as higher growth entrepreneurs. The complementary combination of both knowledge-worker employees (whose jobs have more than doubled in the last three decades, with no signs of that trend slowing,[104] and who are at low to no risk of automation[105]) and job-creating entrepreneurs is needed to improve national economic competitiveness and quality of life.

The strategy and enabling elements of the *IC Framework* are designed to inform disconnected communities how to align and structure new community systems that support economic inclusion and competitiveness. They give guidance to increase the number of resilient economic athletes from disconnected populations and communities within the nation's Innovation Economy priority areas.

METRICS

Inclusive Competitiveness, the *IC Framework,* and the programs and strategic initiatives that support and advance them are an interconnected

104 Josh Zumbrun, "The Rise of Knowledge Workers Is Accelerating Despite the Threat of Automation," *The Wall Street Journal,* May 4, 2016, accessed November 29, 2016, http://blogs.wsj.com/economics/2016/05/04/the-rise-of-knowledge-work-ers-is-accelerating-despite-the-threat-of-automation/.

105 Hasan Bakhshi, Carl Benedikt Frey, and Michael Osborne, "Creativity vs. Robots: The Creative Economy and the Future of Employment," April 2015, accessed September 3, 2016, https://www.nesta.org.uk/sites/default/files/creativity_vs._robots_wv.pdf.

system designed to link with and support the nation's comprehensive Innovation Economy objectives. They are not intended to be isolated, standalone activities. Rather, they should be embedded in and become part and parcel to successful regional, state, and national economic competitiveness strategies. Accordingly, *Inclusive Competitiveness* and the *IC Framework* follow and build on—and do not replace—existing regional, state, and national metrics, with an exclusive focus on measuring the productivity of disconnected populations.

Most incumbent economic competitiveness strategies have done a good job of identifying the best existing and emerging opportunities, and have already won strong buy-in and ownership from stewards of innovation and entrepreneurship ecosystems. They typically measure local or regional performance in areas such as employment and wages in emerging industries and clusters, research and development expenditures, patents, business formation, private capital formation and investment, educational attainment, STEM educational attainment, mergers and acquisitions, initial public offerings, etc.

However, few, if any, have begun to measure either the inputs or outputs of disconnected Americans within these economic competitiveness public objectives. That's where the *IC Framework* comes in, aligning with existing economic competitiveness goals and measuring the productivity of disconnected Americans and their communities within them.

THE MAIN THING

One of *Time* magazine's twenty-five most influential Americans,[106] Stephen R. Covey, is famous for saying: "The main thing is to keep the main thing the main thing." This poignant statement has helped me

---

106 Stephen Covey, "About Steven Covey," accessed November 29, 2016, https://www.stephencovey.com/about/about.php.

keep on track in advancing the *Inclusive Competitiveness* narrative toward action.

Over the past few years, I've observed a new emphasis on technology, innovation, and inclusion. Descriptions such as "inclusive capitalism," "tech diversity," "inclusive innovation," "inclusive entrepreneurship," and "tech inclusion" have gained a measure of traction in places such as London, England, Washington, D.C., and Silicon Valley. These developments are promising. However, as my mother says, "While they are clearly necessary, they also are entirely insufficient." These efforts are necessary because they help put the issue of economic inclusion on the national and global leadership tables for ongoing consideration, planning, investment, and action. They are insufficient because their focus tends to be so far down the opportunity continuum that it is difficult to imagine how they can substantially impact disconnected people and communities.

Case in point: the U.S. is the first and perhaps only nation conceived in capitalism. There are not many who do not know the significance of the date July 4, 1776. However, we should be mindful of another revolutionary event that occurred a few months earlier. On March 9 of the same year, Adam Smith, Scottish social philosopher and political economist, published *The Wealth of Nations.*[107] Serving as a foundational description of free market economics and the first comprehensive system of political economy, it is one of the most influential books ever published on building national economies and wealth. Many of Smith's ideas are rooted in the DNA of America.

One particularly radical view in *The Wealth of Nations* describes much of what we now call capitalism: that wealth lies not in gold but in

---

107 Andrew Beattie, Adam Smith, "The Wealth Of Nations," Investopedia, Updated September 16, 2014, accessed November 29, 2016, http://www.investopedia.com/articles/economics/09/adam-smith-wealth-of-nations.asp

the productive capacity of all people, each seeking to benefit from his or her own labors, and that the flow of goods and services constitutes the ultimate aim and end of economic life.[108] Smith's democratic, egalitarian, and meritocratic view flew in the face of the British aristocracy who centrally held and doled out privileges to merchants, farmers, and working guilds.[109]

Today, America is unquestionably a mixed economy, with strong elements of both free-market capitalism and partial economic control by government over many goods or services, such as education, courts, roads, hospital care, and postal delivery. The government also provides subsidies to agricultural producers and oil, financial, and utility companies.[110]

Generally, we believe in the productive capacity of people, and that they should a) participate in the value they create and b) enjoy a supply-and-demand-based market with restrained and well-considered government interference. It is not always a fair economy, but it is a reasonably efficient economic system in which new jobs and wealth are created regularly.

In our economy there is no centralized, national mechanism to categorically steer or conclusively dole out education and economic opportunity. Rather, by and large, our economy demands, accommodates, and reacts to competitive assets and the energy tends to flow to the best prepared people and enterprises. While I believe it has a moral duty to interact equally and equitably with all assets—something it

---

108 William Welch, "Adam Smith: Capitalism's Founding Father," Vision, 2006, accessed November 26, 2016, http://www.vision.org/visionmedia/biography-adam-smith/868. aspx.

109 Ibid.

110 Sean Ross, "Is the United States considered a market economy or a mixed economy?" Investopedia, March 18, 2015, accessed November 30, 2016, http://www.investopedia. com/ask/answers/031815/united-states-considered-market-economy-or-mixed-economy.asp.

has historically struggled to acknowledge and embrace–our economy is and will remain unyielding in its demands. In essence, the supply of America's best opportunities flows disproportionately, though certainly not exclusively, to the nation's most competitive assets. *Inclusive Competitiveness* creates systems to improve access to those opportunities.

Consequently, if we want disconnected Americans to gain access to and win a fair share of the top future jobs and entrepreneurship opportunities further down the opportunity continuum, then it is important to create sustainable community systems early in the opportunity continuum. These community systems become the portals through which disconnected Americans and their businesses can steadily become more competitive. As discussed above in the *IC Framework* strategy elements, presently, there is little infrastructure in disconnected communities that is organized, operated, and funded to deliver these solutions.

Compounding the absence of community systems in disconnected communities is the preponderance of narrowly tailored, direct-service and place-based programs, such as Empowerment Zones and HUBZones.[111] While beneficial to communities, these programs are generally disconnected from the regional, state, and national economic competitiveness priorities. Moreover, the present focus of "tech inclusion" is in singular programs that build little overall community capacity. Some

---

111   Housing and Urban Development Empowerment Zones (EZ), designated areas of high poverty and unemployment that benefit from tax incentives provided to businesses in the boundaries of the EZ, including tax credits for each of its employees who resides in the EZ. http://portal.hud.gov/hudportal/HUD?src=/hudprograms/empowerment_zones.
Small Business Administration Historically Underutilized Business Zones (HUBZones), promotes economic development and employment growth in distressed areas by providing preferences to improve access to federal contracting opportunities. https://www.sba.gov/contracting/government-contracting-programs/hubzone-program/understanding-hubzone-program

of these programs are trailblazing. However, these programs will not have a significant and enduring impact on disconnected communities as they appear to lack the necessary enabling narrative, policy, strategy, and practice that nurture community systems.

Community systems fulfill a primary need in disconnected communities—over the span of decades—to continually produce, scale, and replicate both effective programs and successful strategic initiatives that address top economic priorities. *Inclusive Competitiveness* builds those community systems.

Take for example the present trend of "inclusive entrepreneurship" that generally cherry-picks the best existing disconnected entrepreneurs for investment. While a great outcome for those select entrepreneurs, this approach is an unsustainable one. There's just *not yet* the bench strength or depth of actual or potential deal flow to realistically sustain these efforts. Instead we need new community systems that can fairly predictably (over an extended period) produce an ongoing flow of entrepreneurs who can successfully compete for such investments. By building this entrepreneurial bench strength in disconnected communities, the *IC Framework* can help deliver more deals and funding options long after the initial "inclusive entrepreneurship" investment cycle.

National and global objectives such as "inclusive capitalism," "tech diversity," "inclusive innovation," and the like are worthwhile themes and activities indeed, but they are not possible to truly realize without first advancing *Inclusive Competitiveness*. It is the *main thing* and should be kept the *main thing*.

CHAPTER 4

SMALL ACTIONS; LARGER IMPACT

Archimedes' Lever

"Give me a firm place to stand, a lever long enough and a prop strong enough, and I will move the Earth."

– ARCHIMEDES, MATHEMATICIAN
AND INVENTOR, C287–C212 BC

Everyone loves success stories, whether it is the result of years of hard work or just a seemingly unbelievable stroke of good luck. But most successful people will tell you that, while luck may have played a small part in the equation, it was their perseverance and hard work that was the key. The same goes for businesses and community organizations: sometimes we look at the explosive growth and impact of these entities and we simply assume that these were overnight successes. Almost invariably when we delve deeper we find it was, in fact, due to smart decisions and intentional actions that built to a critical mass, resulting in exponential growth or far-reaching impact. Take examples such as Google and Amazon, or an emerging company like 4Moms (which designs and manufactures high-end equipment for babies and toddlers), or the success of community organizations like Teach for America (one of the nation's most impactful and most studied educational leadership development organizations) or Harlem Children's Zone® (HCZ®). Their success is the result of a confluence of many factors over a significant amount of time and rarely happenstance.

Many times, our predilection for the romantic notions of "overnight" success ascribes too much to luck and blocks us from acknowledging the vision, commitment, and hard work that has occurred. When it comes to community organizations, oftentimes the important questions are neglected: What is the talent like in these high-performing organizations? What types of investments are necessary for them to succeed? What are the operating models of these organizations? How are these models different from most of those operating in disconnected communities?

The application of Archimedes' Lever as a metaphor for such success is apt: a small lever can easily lift an object—no matter how heavy it is—as long as the ground is firm, the lever is long enough, and the fulcrum is close enough to the object in question. (See the illustration at the beginning of this chapter.) Applied to a community improvement scenario, the lever is the idea, and the prop includes any necessary partners, especially those close to the challenge or opportunity who can assist with implementation. The overall objective is to elicit real change (move the world).

But first, everything begins with a firm place to stand. Without that, there is no leverage. It does not matter how great your lever (idea) is or how strong your prop is (or partners or collaborators are); if you are standing on shaky ground, sinking in mud or quicksand, you cannot achieve your desired outcomes. This explains why enduring organizational impact challenges are found in disconnected communities, which on the whole lack solid platforms.

Top-performing organizations have the funding, operating models, and resources necessary to make a larger impact. However, the type of (and level of) investment from government, philanthropy, individuals, and businesses that will enable these operating models is wanting or altogether absent in disconnected communities. The organizations in these communities look nothing like those market-leading entities (including business accelerators and venture development organizations) present outside these communities. There is also difficulty in attracting and retaining talent in disconnected community organizations that generally cannot keep up with their top-performing counterparts. As a result, the public is often disappointed and those who fund the community's efforts become disenchanted.

Without the right talent, operating models, partnerships, and investments, it does not matter how great the ideas are—achieving optimal community impact is close to impossible.

STRUGGLING IN THE NEW ECONOMY

Many communities that once thrived in the manufacturing and industrial age are continuously struggling in the Innovation Economy. When these ongoing struggles set in, it becomes exceedingly difficult for communities to regain their previous economic preeminence.

However, struggling in this new economy does not need to signal a death knell for the community. Just as communities sometimes tip in a negative direction, they can also reverse the trend, positioning themselves for a turnaround and greater economic prosperity. This is something we will discuss in detail in Chapter 6. At the same time, though, we must not be complacent; we cannot simply hope for positive results and "good luck." Instead, we need to dig deep, ask new and sometimes difficult questions, and make thoughtful decisions based on the answers to those questions.

For example, I once was recruited to lead an organization with a budget of $2.5 million that claimed to annually serve 5,000 people. Organizations of this size of budget in disconnected communities are generally considered to be large and well-funded, with the potential for tremendous impact. When the numbers are broken down, however, the impact was not nearly as impressive. That organization was investing about $500 worth of its services, staff time, and administrative overhead for each person it served.

By contrast, let's look at the HCZ®, an internationally renowned organization that touts itself as "a national model for breaking the cycle of poverty with proven success."[112] During 2015, HCZ® worked with 26,865 youth and adults[113] and had operating expenses of just under $96

---

112 "Fact Sheet," Harlem Children's Zone, accessed November 30, 2016, http://hcz.org/wp-content/uploads/2014/04/FY-2013-FactSheet.pdf.
113 "FY 2015 Report," Harlem Children's Zone, accessed November 30, 2016, http://hcz.org/wp-content/uploads/2016/02/HCZ-FY-2015-Report.pdf.

million.[114] That represents an astounding investment of about $3,600 of organization services, time, talent, and wherewithal per person served by HCZ®—and that is more than seven times what my organization was able to invest (despite it being one of the largest in the city serving disconnected communities).

This opens the door to new inquiries: *How much value in actual services are disconnected community organizations able to deliver to each person they serve, and how much of a difference does it really make?*

At the same time, this scenario begs even larger questions: What actions make a difference to people and communities when it comes to the economy? Is it attaining marketable skills? Starting a business? Or is it understanding how to meet *future* economic challenges—as opposed to mistakenly fixating on the present or past?

Paradoxically, the answer is conditionally all of the above—and none of the above. That is, employable skills, entrepreneurship, and awareness of the global economy are integral ingredients, but these elements alone will not ensure broad, inclusive success. To address these issues—and more—when it comes to meaningful individual and collaborative impact, it is vital to understand Trim Tab Theory.

THE POWER OF TRIM TAB

The trim tab concept, originally introduced by the twentieth century engineer and homespun philosopher R. Buckminster Fuller, described an effective way to use small, highly leveraged actions to achieve outsized results. I think it is fitting to let Fuller explain the process:

---

114 "2014-15 Biennial Report," Harlem Children's Zone, accessed November 30, 2016, http://wac.adef.edgecastcdn.net/80ADEF/hcz.org/wp-content/uploads/2015/11/HCZ-Biennial-Report-2014-2015-single-pages.pdf.

Something hit me very hard once, thinking about what one little man could do. Think of the Queen Mary—the whole ship goes by and then comes the rudder. And there's a tiny thing at the edge of the rudder called a trim tab. It's a miniature rudder. Just moving the little trim tab builds a low pressure that pulls the rudder around. Takes almost no effort at all. So I said that the little individual can be a trim tab … if you're doing dynamic things mentally, the fact is that you can just put your foot out like that and the whole big ship of state is going to go. So I said, call me Trim Tab.

— BUCKMINSTER FULLER

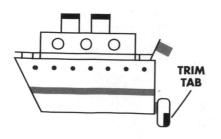

TRIM TAB

This evocative definition illustrates the way people can elicit exponential, positive change for themselves, their communities, and organizations by capitalizing on the power of the trim tab.

While the main job of that large rudder is to turn the ship, it simply cannot do so efficiently and effectively without the high-leverage trim tab. Minus a trim tab, the sheer size and weight of the rudder, along with the water pressure and drag on it, makes the helmsman's task of turning the giant rudder—and thus the ship—nearly impossible.

I like to call people and organizations whose capabilities provide the higher leverage leadership needed to turn a matter of importance in the desired direction Trim Tabbers. That's because their actions significantly increase the achievement potential of a group, considerably enhancing the probability of collaborative success. When people apply

Trim Tab Theory to their lives, communities, or organizations, they not only can deliver more value but also possess the potential to turn something as vast as the economy in a better direction.

Inclusive Competitiveness can be a trim tab of the U.S. economy; it is a small and localized thrust that has the potential to deliver outsized impact to regional and national economies by accessing, equipping, and empowering previously untapped potential of disconnected Americans.

WHO ARE THESE TRIM TABBERS?

Trim Tab Theory requires trim tab talent. *Inclusive Competitiveness* Trim Tabbers are people who:

- Energetically and closely operate throughout disconnected communities,
- Seek to connect the dots to develop, access, and capitalize on new innovation and economic inclusion and competitiveness opportunities, and
- Are committed to ensuring that disconnected Americans emerge as a positive, contributing force in the Innovation Economy.

The pool of Trim Tabbers may be fairly small given the need for individuals whose personality and drive matches the aforementioned list. Here's just a sampling of some of the traits and characteristics that most Trim Tabbers share:

- **Entrepreneurial spirit.** Similar to business entrepreneurs, they treat innovation and economic inclusion and competitiveness challenges in disconnected communities like market opportunities requiring market solutions.
- **Courage.** They possess courage born of strong convictions and vision.

- **Passion.** Their energy, along with a conspicuous public presence, allows them to lead by influence and persuasion. In the end, they garner the support of diverse groups of people with the intention of getting them to understand, accept, and act upon new ideas.

- **Competitive nature.** Because of their competitive nature, they are naturally risk-astute—as opposed to risk-averse or risky. They are willing to step out (and step through) their fear and the possible judgment of others to fulfill their mission.

- **Strong communication skills.** How they achieve the desired exponential impact depends on their ability to effectively connect with a broad range of constituents to build relations among and between people in the following sectors: business, government, economic development, philanthropy, education, media, and community organizations.

- **Solution-oriented nature.** They are value-adders who understand the needs of disconnected America. Informed by their real, on-the-ground experience, they constantly assess challenges and achieve innovation and economic inclusion and competitiveness solutions among disconnected populations, as well as create new opportunities. They greatly enhance the value of funders' money by catalyzing, leading, driving, and managing the development of new community systems and implementation of higher impact projects, programs, and strategic initiatives that have a multiplying effect. Best of all, they can detect and mitigate tipping points, which allows them to perceive and accelerate transformation points.

THE ANATOMY OF A TRIM
TAB ORGANIZATION

The functional expression of Trim Tab Theory is the Trim Tab Organization (TTO), which succeeds if it attracts and retains trim tab talent. Now, let's take a closer look at organizations that reflect Trim Tab Theory. These are entities whose operational approach to achieve their mission impact is based on aggregating key resources; organizing those resources into actionable measures; and highly leveraging those resources to deliver exponential impact, as opposed to only smaller, incremental outcomes. In doing these things, TTOs create conditions for community change.

When enough TTO leadership and activities are aligned to make an impact in the marketplace, we witness a Trim Tab Movement. This is characterized by a series of high-leverage, organized actions at the local level that ultimately can achieve a massive, national, perhaps global, impact over an extended period of time.

Historically, movements begin locally and later connect with like minds and interests more broadly to advance their agendas. For instance, the gay rights movement has become an issue with considerable and sustained support–but twenty years ago, this was not the case. So, what caused fragmented local groups to gain enough momentum to create a nationwide movement that is no longer a political wedge issue? Basically, the evolution of a movement boils down to the following levers:

- Local groups catalyze, grow, align, and connect with one another.
- People utilize technology and any other communication tools, such as social media, to disseminate the word and garner support.
- Supporters publicize the agenda in a compelling way to elicit activism, financial backing, political support, etc.

- The movement begins to pick up momentum, resulting in even greater awareness for a new narrative and progress toward the desired action.
- Socio-political policy shifts occur that sustain and strengthen the movement.

But how can this shift happen in a community, economically speaking? Let's take the TTO down to its bare bones to better understand what makes it so powerful. These organizations develop and support local initiatives that:

- Require partners to act together,
- Are sustainable; once they've begun they can be kept going, and
- Can improve and exponentially (rather than incrementally) increase their impact.

Once these shifts happen, the community's projects, programs, and strategic initiatives can achieve more of their desired impact.

In the past, most people subscribed to the belief that traditional, direct-service community organizations alone were the best way to spark and empower local action—but this is no longer true. While needs have grown, providers have changed, funding has become more unstable, and the economy is continually being reinvented, there remains a profound lack of alignment with the Innovation Economy among most direct-service providers, especially those in disconnected communities. Unfortunately, since the War on Poverty and Model Cities Program of the 1960s, the absence of evolution has resulted in these communities having few organizational leadership mechanisms to help them keep up with the changing times.

The traditional methods of organizing disconnected communities (e.g., primarily through direct social, education, and human service providers and small business development) are not enough to either catalyze or sustain economic prosperity. However, Trim Tab Theory and the TTO model address these changing needs in the Innovation Economy as a way to help breathe new life into disconnected communities. TTOs possess this unique potential because they are organized differently from traditional community organizations and ad hoc systems. A well-run TTO can continue to provide more traditional services and, at the same time, deliver expanded community impact, allowing them to reach far larger numbers of people than ever before.

The TTO is a like a living being and consists of the following:

- It is a carefully nurtured, well-connected body made up of Trim Tabbers (with friends in key places).
- It has a highly flexible workforce (extensively leveraging consulting talent and expertise) that can grow bigger or shrink smaller as needed, based on real market needs and demands.
- It goes beyond narrowly serving individual citizens and helps to create conditions conducive to community success in the twenty-first century.

Foundational to all these characteristics is an organization with a vision of high-leverage impact. When the Internet arrived, most people thought it was just a nifty tool for finding information if we could not find it any other way. Now, practically everyone leverages the Internet to stay connected to family and friends, hold conversations, conduct business, and create our own virtual communities. When great-grandparents are using iPads to FaceTime their families, change has arrived! In the same way, it is time for the traditional community organization to transform. Exercising high leverage is the key.

MOVING FROM YESTERDAY TO TODAY

Traditional community organizations have a long history of making a difference in people's lives. However, it is clear now that what these groups do—and more importantly, *how* they have done it in the past—is no longer sufficient. Many organization leaders have rightly concluded that they need to do more, lead more, and contribute in new and more productive ways.

There are several reasons for this new thinking:

- Funding for community organizations tends to be restricted to specific programs. Because of that, these entities lack needed flexibility and may not be able to respond quickly to new needs, demands, and opportunities.

- People increasingly expect their community's local organizations to deliver solutions in a wide variety of areas.

- Because these direct-service community organizations are so labor- and cost-intensive, their ability to exponentially impact the citizens of that area is constrained. Even those with larger staff numbers and budget amounts, relative to disconnected community organization standards, are saddled with a no-win proposition: either provide larger numbers of people with fewer quality services or serve smaller numbers with greater quality. These communities need high quality services that are delivered to lots of people.

- As the American economy becomes more knowledge-based, the need for empowerment and expanding community impact is progressively building. To enhance prosperity, direct-service organizations cannot by themselves adequately support and help grow a community. Instead, today's communities need to build sustainable, economically competitive community infrastructure and work together to acquire more resources that will improve education attainment and create businesses and jobs.

Organizations that become TTOs will be most ready to provide leadership and services in our new reality of fewer resources and more demands. What we need are evolved *systems* of talent, networks, and collaboration if we are going to achieve high-impact results.

THE BASICS: VISION AND MISSION

Every great organizational model has a compelling vision and mission. So it is with the TTO model, whose prototypical mission, describing its day-to-day work, can be summed up as:

To exponentially increase community impact by attracting and retaining talent needed to build systems that promote sustained prosperity through a blend of useful direct citizen services and collaborative community leadership.

Furthermore, the TTO vision—or what the organization wants to achieve over time—is:

To be the best points of entry and outreach for leadership that empowers citizens to develop and contribute their full potential, resulting in increased social, educational, and economic inclusion and competitiveness and improved lives.

Let's break down the key elements of the TTO mission:

- *Exponentially increase* means we serve many more people than before.
- *Systems* refers to community-led structures and mechanisms used by citizens, community organizations and groups to interact,

coordinate, and deliver their responses to the challenges, needs, and opportunities affecting their communities.

- *Sustained prosperity* means supporting enduring growth and development in education, entrepreneurship, innovation, productivity, employment, and standard of living.
- *Direct citizen services* are those delivered directly to individuals and families.
- *Collaborative community leadership* means people work together to accomplish and surpass meaningful objectives—exponentially.

And these are the elements of the TTO vision:

- *Points of entry and outreach* refers to the starting point for citizens to reach in to connect to community systems and, conversely, for community systems to reach out to connect to citizens.
- *Empowering* is defined as helping people see and realize their ability to make an impact.
- *Develop and contribute* means people growing the capacity to play an important part in achieving results.
- *Full potential* is all you can become.
- *Social, educational, and economic inclusion and competitiveness* means taking advantage of the many cultures and segments of our nation to successfully compete in today's global, knowledge-based economy.

This is not about radically changing any group's core purpose, but thinking in new ways about *how* the purpose can be achieved. The TTO model provides the means.

Taken together, the vision and mission are the heart of any TTO. They move us to action. They hold our store of community knowledge.

They allow other groups to help us achieve the impact we want and need. They show us the kind of leadership needed to achieve *exponential impact* for ourselves, our communities, and America.

THE TTO IS A "SIMPLE" ORGANIZATION

In his book, *Good to Great* (2001), organizational expert Jim Collins says that organizations are either "complex" or "simple." *Complex* organizations draw up complicated strategies to reach a number of goals all at the same time. Because of this, they are scattered all over the place, never integrating their thinking and actions into an overall, unifying vision.

On the flipside, *simple* organizations hold a single, central vision aligned to their beliefs and experiences—a North Star—to guide them. They make complex things easy to understand and accomplish: they follow a single concept that guides everything. Similarly, under the TTO model, any traditional community organization can become *simple*.

So, these are the *simple* things that feed the body of a TTO:

- *Talent*: The TTO is led by Trim Tabbers.
- *Expertise:* The TTO is the local starting point for people working together to progressively increase community impact.
- *Fuel:* The TTO taps into various forms of local wealth—individual, corporate, philanthropic, community, and government sources.
- *Engine:* The TTO will be known as an important place that pulls together disconnected Americans to bring trailblazing ideas to life through their actions.
- *Service:* The TTO keeps the basic purpose of traditional community organizations they have always had, but fulfills it in a *different way*—a way that results in consistently growing impact.

RISE TO THE CHALLENGE

A simple game of bean bag toss a few years ago had me thinking of parallels to disconnected communities:

- You can have a pretty true aim with insufficient power and you miss your mark, and
- You can have a lot of power, even too much, but without good aim your efforts will amount to little.

Sometimes, we come up with the idea for a great program that affects disconnected populations, but the scope and impact is too narrow (accurate beanbag toss, but short of the hole). Other times, we throw lots of money and resources at an endeavor without ever realizing desired results (throwing the beanbag with plenty of power while missing the mark). Like my game of beanbag toss, creating exponential impact in disconnected communities is more difficult than it looks. However, with practice and guidance we can create the requisite conditions to learn the game and become proficient at it. This may involve new strategies (discussed throughout this book), along with a willingness to make a shift in mindset. Both open-mindedness and more effective strategies will help communities to overcome their persistent challenges and begin to make a radical transformation.

By creating policies, strategies, and systems that focus on *process* in addition to *product*—or programs—we will begin to see new conditions emerge that can help move communities in a positive direction. Unfortunately, at this point in time, these models—as implemented through TTOs—are rare to find among the disconnected.

To elicit true change, traditional community leadership groups—in the form of governmental agencies, community organizations, education, human services, and philanthropies—need to refresh (not necessarily change) their purpose and update their mission, vision, and operating models. To best help individuals and communities prepare to successfully compete in today's economic environment, we will need to combine elements of both traditional and trim tab thinking and doing to create a new way.

It is important to note that this is an asset-based approach and not one merely focusing on deficits. Instead of concentrating on what the community may *not* have, it is critical to determine what the community *does* have and how that can connect to its new objectives. No matter how much a community is struggling, there are still assets to be found—whether it is through the people, infrastructure, location, or any other positive element that can be sourced and leveraged.

To illustrate this point: Many market-leading Innovation Economy assets are located in urban areas, and as such many disconnected communities would have locational proximity on their side. A community may already have, or have access to, a resource or talent pool that they are simply not aware exists; it is possible that there are nearby organizations, institutions, and other entities that might be useful to the community—even though no one ever has taken advantage of the benefits of having that particular resource in their own backyard! Communities can access and leverage these assets in fresh and new ways. The key is to effectively tap into them to benefit the community members.

There is no single universal remedy, yet blending traditional leadership with Trim Tab Theory is an important first step. Then, as the momentum begins to shift, the concepts of tipping and transformation points (as discussed in Chapter 6) will come into play. As a result, it then becomes possible to slow down, stop, and even reverse the negative forces of economic decline that threaten many communities. In essence,

TTOs help create community systems that *connect* disconnected Americans to emerging and leading opportunities. Ultimately, this new way of thinking and doing can help transform a community so that it can realize its potential to grow, thrive, and experience true prosperity in this ever-changing, modern world.

CHAPTER 5

THE OHIO EXPERIENCE

OHIO: THE NATIONAL BELLWETHER

A bellwether can be defined as something that serves as a leader or leading indicator of future trends. And according to Eric Ostermeier—a research associate at University of Minnesota Humphrey School of Public Affairs' Center for the Study of Politics and Governance—there is no better national bellwether than Ohio:

> There is one state that has consistently mimicked the pulse of the national electorate more than any other during the 20th and 21st centuries – Ohio. Simply put, Ohio has been the most accurate political thermometer across the 50 states when used to take the temperature of the national electorate over the decades. During the 112 years of presidential elections since the turn of the 20th century through 2012, the Buckeye State's vote for the winning candidate has deviated less than four points from the national popular vote in an astounding

26 of 29 cycles and by less than two points in 17 of these. Since 1964, Ohio has been particularly in sync with the national electorate, not only for being the only state to back the winning candidate in every cycle during this 13-cycle span but also voting for the winning nominee within an average of just 1.3 points of the national vote. [115]

In 2016, Ohio extended what is by far the longest streak in the U.S. of voting with the national winner to fourteen straight elections, with the next closest being Florida, which picked the winner in six straight elections, followed by North Carolina with five. [116]

A surprisingly diverse state—with everything from big cities to rolling fields, rustbelt industries to Appalachian poverty—Ohio is a microcosm of America. [117] The upshot is that whatever is happening in Ohio is likely either already happening in every other state or is on its way there. My work with the Ohio Department of Higher Education strongly reflects the challenges and opportunities of our nation's diverse demographic and geographic landscape. It has reinforced that the processes applied, and the experiences and resultant findings of that work, are applicable to disconnected communities throughout the U.S.

---

115 Dr. Eric Ostermeier, "As Ohio Goes, So Goes the Nation," Smart Politics, June 10, 2015, accessed November 30, 2016, http://editions.lib.umn.edu/smartpolitics/2015/06/10/as-ohio-goes-so-goes-the-natio/.

116 Rick Exner, "Trump had at least 70 percent of the vote in 30 Ohio counties; 6 takeaways from Ohio's 2016 presidential vote," The Cleveland Plain Dealer, November 9, 2016, http://www.cleveland.com/election-results/index.ssf/2016/11/trump_had_at_least_70_percent.html.

117 "The swing states: Ohio, The big, bellwether battlefield," The Economist, July 31, 2008, accessed November 30, 2016, http://www.economist.com/node/11848408.

INNOVATION BELLWETHER: OHIO THIRD FRONTIER

According to the report *Making an Impact: Assessing the Benefits of Ohio's Investment in Technology-Based Economic Development Programs*, Ohio's thinking about issues related to the to what we now call the Innovation Economy and how the state could play a catalytic role in its development dates back to the early 1980s. True to its bellwether character, Ohio was among the first states to meaningfully invest in Innovation Economy development. In 1983, Ohio's legislature created the Thomas Edison Program, a state-funded initiative to encourage universities to cooperate with businesses. Its aim was to link research and technology with startup companies and other business initiatives. The Edison program has supported the establishment of nine business incubators, seven technology centers, and "seed development fund projects" across the state.[118] The state's second major endeavor, nearly twenty years later, was to put in place a comprehensive set of programs to:

- Support world-class research from the University System of Ohio and other higher education institutions aligned with industry platforms,
- Encourage collaborative research and commercialization activities, and
- Spur new technology company formation.

---

118 *Best Practices in State and Regional Innovation Initiatives: Competing in the 21st Century,* (Washington, DC: The National Research Council of the National Academies, The National Academies Press, 2013), 114.

This $2.1 billion set of programs—the largest development initiative ever undertaken in the state[119]—is known as the Ohio Third Frontier (OTF Initiative). The name describes Ohio's economic evolution. The first frontier was agricultural; the second frontier was industrial; and the third frontier is the knowledge and technology-driven Innovation Economy.

The *Making an Impact* study records several major accomplishments of the OTF Initiative. Notably:

- A dramatic increase in the availability of early-stage capital in Ohio,
- Improvement of the environment for Ohio technology entrepreneurs,
- Improvement in research and development collaboration among the University System of Ohio, other higher education and research institutions, and industry,
- Employment growth in Ohio's technology sector,
- Contribution to the diversification and competitiveness of Ohio manufacturers,
- Recruitment of non-Ohio companies to the state, and
- A newly charted course for Ohio consistent with successful Innovation Economy growth in other regions.

Perhaps the most important effect of these investments is the development of the Ohio innovation and entrepreneurship ecosystem: an effective, integrated system for supporting innovation and new enterprise and job creation at all levels and by all key actors including companies, entrepreneurs, universities, research institutions, and federal labs. It is now well-known that Ohio's capacity for innovation and new job creation depends on an effective ecosystem that involves many elements, including:

---

119 Ibid.

- A large and diverse base of talented people,
- Research and development,
- Financing,
- Market pull,
- A supportive policy environment, and other essentials.

Any single element not optimally producing can cripple the overall performance of the ecosystem. Unfortunately, when it comes to nurturing a large and diverse talent base—specifically as it relates to disconnected Ohioans—the state's ecosystem has not performed. This impediment undermines prospects for Ohio's increased long-term economic competitiveness.

CONNECTING DISCONNECTED OHIOANS

The OTF Initiative is an example of Ohio's extraordinary leadership in the Innovation Economy. There are two provisions of the law governing the OTF Initiative that are especially important for *Inclusive Competitiveness*:

- The minority and rural outreach sections of the Ohio Revised Code mandate the OTF Initiative conduct significant outreach activities to include minorities and rural populations in the various projects and initiatives sponsored, funded, encouraged, or otherwise promoted by the program.
- Ohio law requires the OTF Initiative to direct outreach activities at faculty and students involved in science and engineering disciplines, professional scientists and engineers, technical assistance providers, the investment community, minority-owned

businesses, and minority entrepreneurs.[120]

OHIO DEPARTMENT OF HIGHER EDUCATION AND INCLUSIVE COMPETITIVENESS

The Ohio Department of Higher Education (ODHE), is a cabinet-level agency for the governor that oversees higher education for the state. The agency is directed by its chancellor, who is a member of the governor of Ohio's cabinet. The chancellor, with the advice of the nine-member board, provides policy guidance to the governor and the Ohio General Assembly, advocates for the University System of Ohio, and carries out state higher education policy.

The OTF Initiative established a greater role for higher education in preparing and equipping all Ohioans to meet both the workforce and job creation needs of the state in the twenty-first century. New technology-based products and services, companies, industries, and jobs will reach the market with the added help of well-trained and highly

---

120 Ohio Revised Code 184.17 Outreach activities - minority defined. As used in sections 184.171, 184.172, and 184.173 of the Revised Code, "minority" means an individual who is a United States citizen and who is a member of one of the following economically disadvantaged groups: Blacks or African Americans, American Indians, Hispanics or Latinos, and Asians. http://codes.ohio.gov/orc/184.17.

Ohio Revised Code 184.171 Minorities to be included in outreach activities and projects. The Third Frontier Commission shall conduct outreach activities described in section 184.172 of the Revised Code that seek to include minorities in the various projects and initiatives sponsored, funded, encouraged, or otherwise promoted by the commission. The commission shall direct the activities at faculty and students involved in science and engineering disciplines, professional scientists and engineers, technical assistance providers, the investment community, minority-owned businesses, and minority entrepreneurs. http://codes.ohio.gov/orc/184.171.

Ohio Revised Code 184.18 Outreach activities to rural areas. (2) "Rural area" means any area of this state not located within a metropolitan statistical area. (B) The Third Frontier Commission shall conduct outreach activities that seek to include rural areas in the various projects and initiatives sponsored, funded, encouraged, or otherwise promoted by the commission. (1) Working with all institutions of higher education in the state to support faculty and students involved in science and engineering who focus on third frontier projects and initiatives in rural areas. http://codes.ohio.gov/orc/184.18.

skilled innovators and entrepreneurs. In turn, the success of those companies will increase the demand for new, intrapreneurial workers (people within companies who start new, value-generating initiatives for their organizations). This intentional economic activity, catalyzed in large part by the state's investment, introduced an urgent need for higher education to respond. It does so by developing a healthy flow of economic athletes through the dual pipelines of a tech-ready workforce and higher growth, tech-driven entrepreneurs.

As discussed in Chapter 2, after my presentation to the ODHE about education and economic inclusion and competitiveness, the agency created the Subcommittee on *Inclusive Competitiveness*. I became a consultant to the project, providing expertise, energy, and vision.

To determine the performance of disconnected Ohioans in the state's Innovation Economy, the subcommittee spent more than six months examining national, state, and regional quantitative economic and education data. This was supplemented by information gathered from interviewing representatives of the University System of Ohio, state government programs, STEM / STEAM-focused education programs and initiatives, minority- and rural-serving organizations, and regional technology- and innovation-based economic development organizations.

Of crucial note is that women were not specifically defined in the OTF Initiative governing legislation as a "minority." However, the subcommittee believed that Ohio women were a vital untapped source of an innovative, intrapreneurial workforce and entrepreneurial enterprise talent pool that could enhance the state's education and economic competitiveness. And, thus, the subcommittee included women in its definition of disconnected Ohioans.

PRIMACY OF POLICY

The ODHE was energized by prospects that new thought and advocacy, which focused on inclusively improving the state's productivity, could positively impact Ohio's "policymaking class" and result in a new education and economic inclusion and competitiveness policy regime. Broadly-defined policy is the *substantive breakthrough* needed to create and sustain new programs and strategic initiatives to connect disconnected Ohioans to the Innovation Economy.

Following the *IC Framework*, described in Chapter 3, the ODHE agreed that policy and the "policymaking class" referred to a much larger set of organizations and interests other than purely municipal, county, state, and federal governmental actors.

The ODHE recognized the need and opportunity to catalyze influencers in Ohio to lead the way. New policy expressions were needed to secure the necessary conditions for sustained actions and investments that marshal resources to improve connectivity and productivity.

POLICY AND STRATEGY FIRST

Importantly—and in a stark departure from the conventional approaches—the ODHE subcommittee understood that the force of policy and supporting strategy were the essential first steps to build an inclusive Innovation Economy. Policy and strategy are needed to enable the formation and attraction of the financial investment needed to further extend the benefits of twenty-first century opportunities to disconnected Ohioans.

In the *Art of War*, Chinese general, military strategist, and philosopher Sun Tzu wrote: "Therefore, a victorious army first obtains conditions for victory, then seeks to do battle. A defeated army first seeks to do battle, then obtains conditions for victory."

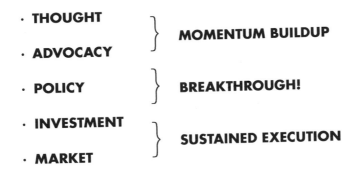

- **THOUGHT** } **MOMENTUM BUILDUP**
- **ADVOCACY**
- **POLICY** } **BREAKTHROUGH!**
- **INVESTMENT** } **SUSTAINED EXECUTION**
- **MARKET**

By following a *policy and strategy first* objective, policymakers can provide critical leadership to *first obtain conditions* (policy and strategy) necessary for economic inclusion and competitiveness. A coordinated and concerted approach must be instituted to replace the usual practice where those deeply committed to these matters frantically run around in disconnected communities desperately trying "to get something done" without the requisite resources.

Unfortunately, customary economic inclusion methods are more ad hoc and do not incorporate a competitiveness dimension. They have resulted in a national collection of disparate programs serving disconnected Americans that are not connected to our top education and economic opportunities.

From my experience, what usually happens when matters of economic inclusion garner attention in a city, region, or state, the policymakers–business, community, government, and philanthropic leaders–will convene a big meeting on the subject. There is lots of good talk and good intentions. Then, in exasperation, a leading policymaker, perhaps a major company CEO, will explicitly declare something like this: "We all know the problems, let's just go out there and get to work!"

Without the development of a guiding North Star policy or strategy and no commitment to fostering new community systems that support economic inclusion, attendees just "go out there and get to work." What happens is a doubling down on isolated programs that don't connect to the Innovation Economy. The end result is even more disparate programs that are connected to neither enduring policy nor strategy and do not reflect the top economic opportunities.

Demonstrable education and economic inclusion investment never, *ever* precede the clear expression of policy and real strategy. Instead, policy and strategy come before investment, and then market leaders and activists can be best ignited to step forward to get things done.

The right policy and strategy can cultivate inclusive and competitive regional innovation and entrepreneurship ecosystems that generate more impactful programs and strategic initiatives. These developments will position U.S. cities, regions, states, and the nation as a whole to be global leaders in improving the productivity of disconnected populations in the Innovation Economy.

Without question, new behaviors in the Ohio market were needed to create, sustain, and ultimately achieve the desired education and economic inclusion and competitiveness impact. New policy and strategy were the mechanisms to ignite them.

SUBCOMMITTEE PROCESS

To fulfill its charge to seek input from a diverse array of stakeholders, the subcommittee travelled throughout Ohio. There followed several regional stakeholder forums across the state, with nearly 125 participants from K-12 and higher education, tech- and innovation-based economic development, incubators and accelerators, government, and philanthropy. The stakeholder forums examined the status of various statewide efforts to:

- Incorporate disconnected Ohioans into the OTF Initiative and regional programs targeted at creating new technology-based companies,
- Inclusively support existing industries to create globally competitive products and services,
- Develop more underrepresented STEM / STEAM-based entrepreneurs, and
- Grow and diversify the talent pipeline in STEM / STEAM-related fields.

Stakeholder forum participants gave ten- to fifteen-minute presentations. They were invited to engage in open dialogue regarding their experiences and efforts to aid the inclusion of disconnected Ohioans in the Innovation Economy.

Moreover, participants provided progress reports on those policy and programmatic initiatives that were designed to attract, expose, and prepare disconnected Ohioans for the Innovation Economy. Of particular interest to the subcommittee were efforts that addressed one or more of the following:

- Proposition of new structures, policies, and practices that would dramatically improve disconnected Ohioans' employment and job creation access, opportunities, and outcomes,
- Identification of the most important factors and practices leading to improved productivity of disconnected Ohioans in the Innovation Economy,

- Assessment of current limitations, policies, practices, and barriers regarding university collaborations with organizations and institutions serving disconnected Ohioans,

- Specification of the current level of productivity of disconnected Ohioans, in terms of STEM education attainment, research, commercialization and technology transfer activities and entrepreneurship, and establishment of aspirational statewide goals,

- Recommendation of strategies that have the potential to improve university collaborations with organizations and institutions serving disconnected Ohioans in the planning and execution of their Innovation Economy activities,

- Delineation of the resources and incentives that could accelerate university collaborations with organizations and institutions serving disconnected Ohioans that are focused on the Innovation Economy, and

- Highlighting of opportunities for infusing a culture of *Inclusive Competitiveness* grounded in learning and performance within the University System of Ohio.

The ODHE process was the first time in Ohio, and was perhaps the first time in the nation, that a government-sanctioned group travelled the state exploring the performance and productivity of disconnected Americans in the twenty-first century economy.

OVERALL THEME

One theme repeatedly surfaced during every subcommittee stakeholder forum that should inform disconnected community efforts throughout the U.S. to adopt and implement *Inclusive Competitiveness* policies, strategies, and practices. It can be distilled into this question: "*Haven't we done this before?*"

Resolving this primary question was vital to the subcommittee's work as the answer provides clarity of purpose and direction. The response was clear and unequivocal: we have not done this before. Despite the Ohio law mandating the OTF Initiative to conduct outreach activities to disconnected Ohioans, there was (and still is) not an identifiable economic inclusion and competitiveness strategy focused on the Innovation Economy at either the state or regional level.

This is an important consideration for disconnected communities, which are served by a rich and diverse set of not-for-profits, as discussed earlier in Chapter 2. These organizations typically provide direct services to residents, often with a focus on areas such as education, human, and social services. Moreover, the business services provided are overwhelmingly focused on areas such as lifestyle businesses (created primarily with the aim of sustaining a particular level of personal income), construction, and myriad dimensions of supplier diversity.

The ODHE subcommittee was adamant not to allow stakeholder forums to devolve into discussions of issues concerning traditional "minority economic development." It aligned—or persuasively realigned—and directed all participants to address the issues of improving the performance and productivity of disconnected Ohioans in, and connecting them to, the state's Innovation Economy priorities.

While the State of Ohio does provide a good portfolio of minority business service and support offerings, there is a distinct absence in its policy and strategy of the explicit language designed to foster connections to leading Innovation Economy opportunities. That which is expressly missing from minority-focused programs includes, but is not limited to, the following key terms, concepts, and phrases excerpted from the OTF Initiative:

- Accelerate the growth of technology companies
- Retain and attract the best and the brightest talent
- Focus on the professional development of young entrepreneurs with the necessary ambition to commercialize new technologies
- Link promising new ventures with early-stage investment capital
- Significantly increase the technology-based entrepreneurial commercialization outcomes
- Focus the effort on strategic technology-based sectors that offer exceptional economic development prospects
- Represent a comprehensive, coordinated network of high-value services and assistance providers that is visible and easily accessible to technology-based entrepreneurs and small tech-based companies
- Tightly integrate sources of deal flow, entrepreneurial support, and capital to effectively grow technology-based entrepreneurial commercialization outcomes
- Accelerate the development and growth of the biomedical, advanced materials, and fuel cell industries
- Support R&D that addresses the technical and cost barriers to commercialization
- Attract leading research talent that can contribute to the growth of research centers of excellence within academic institutions that support economic development priorities of the state
- Advance scientifically unique applied research projects that can sustain the development of new, innovative products, and
- Create world-class research and technology development centers designed to accelerate the pace of commercialization.

RECURRING THEMES

During the stakeholder forums several other themes often surfaced which provide additional helpful insights about the challenges and opportunities for those who want to improve the prospects for success of disconnected Americans in the Innovation Economy. These themes are indicated below. For more detailed descriptions of these themes, visit www.scaleuppartners.com. You will be able to download a copy of the report of the ODHE Subcommittee on *Inclusive Competitiveness*.

1. **Lack of Awareness:** Awareness of Ohio's Innovation Economy was nearly nonexistent among disconnected Ohioans. Moreover, the state had done almost nothing to implement its own governing law mandating the $2.1 billion OTF Initiative to reach out to these Ohioans.

2. **Absence of Connecting Organizational Functions:** There were few to no community organizational mechanisms aggregating, organizing, and leveraging disparate resources that can help disconnected Ohioans grow and sustain their contributions to the Innovation Economy.

3. **Higher Education and Innovation Organization Alignment Opportunity:** There was early, yet strong alignment among Ohio's higher education institutions and regional technology- and innovation-based economic development (T/IBED) organizations. They agreed that there should be new, narrowly focused economic inclusion and competitiveness enabling policies, strategies, practices, and metrics to complement and bolster the state's and regions' broader Innovation Economy agenda.

4. **Need to Push and Pull:** The stakeholder forums made clear the need for two-way movement—derived from new policies, strat-

egies, investments, practices, and metrics—such that awareness of opportunities is intentionally "pushed to" those disconnected from the state's Innovation Economy stewards and funders, while also intentionally "pulling in" these Ohioans to connect to the opportunities made available.

5. **New Relationships Build Bridges:** Ohio's new *Inclusive Competitiveness* thrust should be committed to nurturing strong relationships among K-12, higher education, and T/IBED organizations throughout the state so they can effectively engage, empower, and connect disconnected communities to the state and nation's Innovation Economy. To cultivate connections aligned with regional opportunities, new relationships should be fostered with other stakeholders in the Eight Communities of Influence (discussed in detail in Chapter 8 of this book), such as philanthropy, social, education, and human services organizations, and economic-focused organizations that serve disconnected Ohioans.

6. **Traditional Economic Inclusion Efforts Retain Existing Economic Value; New Efforts are Needed to Generate New Economic Value:** Traditional economic inclusion efforts are largely designed to access and retain existing economic value in Ohio (primarily through government and corporate contracting) for longer periods, circulating and spreading its impact to more people and communities throughout regions of the state. A new thrust must be developed to connect disconnected citizens to the Innovation Economy and create *fully* inclusive regional and statewide innovation and entrepreneurship ecosystems that generate new economic value and grow new enterprises that create jobs.

7. **Widely Differing Investment and Expectations:** Throughout Ohio, and likely throughout the U.S. generally, economic inclusion has not received the same level of scrutiny, study, strategy development, and evaluation as have other areas of the state's economy. Moreover, improving the economic competitiveness of disconnected Ohioans has gained little attention and practically no investment. The needle of economic inclusion and competitiveness will move proportionately with the investment of human and financial capital and other resources devoted to moving it.

REPORT RECOMMENDATIONS ON INCLUSIVE COMPETITIVENESS

The ODHE urged the chancellor to employ all the powers available to his office under the Ohio Revised Code to publicly advocate for overarching education and economic inclusion and competitiveness policies, strategies, practices, and metrics to ensure that disconnected citizens can win in Ohio's Innovation Economy. Though an advisory position, the chancellor's leadership sets the stage and offers the best means for filling a void that is necessary to bolster the economic competitiveness of the state.

The following are the subcommittee's recommendations, with supporting rationale:

1. **Encourage the University System of Ohio and other higher education institutions to introduce and integrate** *Inclusive Competitiveness* **economic narratives in schools, institutions, and communities throughout the state, with a strong focus on disconnected areas.** Much work needs to be done to make the invisible Innovation Economy opportunities visible throughout

the state. New economic narratives are needed in schools and communities to shine light on existing opportunities. However, to offer only new Innovation Economy programs—to those Ohioans who have little community economic narrative that connects them to such programs—is an insufficient response. To facilitate connections to these programs, new economic narratives must be concurrently espoused and embedded in these communities. These narratives should be focused on multi- and interdisciplinary education approaches, job creation, higher growth entrepreneurship, and forming and attracting private investment capital to fuel new enterprise and job growth.

2. **Encourage the University System of Ohio and other higher education institutions to promote inter- and multidisciplinary economic development.** Ohio needs economic development focused on bringing together partners that traditionally have not been involved in T/IBED. In addition to the outstanding existing players—higher education, T/IBED organizations, researchers, higher growth entrepreneurs, and investors—outreach also should be made to social, human, and education services organizations in areas serving disconnected Ohioans. To invite contributions from these diverse organizations and areas of focus that have deep and frequent contact with disconnected Ohioans is to create balance and integration. Without their involvement, achieving broad inclusion and increased competitiveness will be more difficult, if not impossible.

3. **Encourage continued support for the Choose Ohio First Scholarship Program.** During the 127th General Assembly, the Ohio legislature strengthened education in the state by leading

the efforts to create the Choose Ohio First Scholarship with the provision of $100 million in STEMM (science, technology, engineering mathematics, and medicine) scholarship funds to Ohio students attending Ohio colleges and universities. The program is part of the state's strategic effort to significantly strengthen Ohio's K-12 education pipeline to productivity and position the state for sustained success in Innovation Economy markets such as aerospace, advanced manufacturing, medicine, and computer technology.

4. **Collaborate with the Ohio Department of Education to foster articulation and dissemination of *Inclusive Competitiveness* narratives to K-12 educators via educational service centers (ESCs) that are recognized providers of professional development.** Encourage ESCs to provide professional development to improve teacher understanding, instruction, and student learning about Ohio's Innovation Economy, including regional and statewide innovation and entrepreneurship ecosystems, industry clusters, and emerging technology sectors. This approach would activate education systems closest to disconnected Ohio students. ESCs are distributed across the state and serve schools in their respective areas. They can use their insights of the strengths and needs of the K-12 system to positively impact and improve Innovation Economy instruction and student achievement outcomes.

5. **Encourage continued and increasing support for the Believe in Ohio Youth STEM Commercialization and Entrepreneurship Program.** The blend of STEM education and entrepreneurship aligns with Ohio's twenty-first century imperative to both fill

and create new jobs. While Ohio youth show interest in entre-preneurship, too many lack strong interest in STEM education. STEM is seen as the gateway to creating successful higher growth, tech-based startups. So, stronger investment to increase the interest levels of Ohio youth toward STEM and entrepreneurship will ensure that they understand where the opportunities are. It will also strengthen the K-12 and higher educational gateway through which they should pass to access those opportunities.

6. **Encourage the Third Frontier Commission to improve its efforts, as set out in the OTF Initiative regulations regarding minority and rural outreach, and to enlarge the scope of outreach to include women.** The Third Frontier Commission should comple-ment the state's existing OTF Initiative focus areas by exploring, selecting, and prioritizing Innovation Economy areas that promote widespread growth and development throughout Ohio. The commission should include in all OTF Initiative programs (and other support focused on the Innovation Economy) the expectation that individuals and companies receiving state support participate in *Inclusive Competitiveness* activities that further the goals of economic inclusion and competitiveness throughout the state.

Launched in 2002, the OTF Initiative has earned continued support of:

- The people of Ohio, who twice voted in favor,
- Three successive governors, Taft, Strickland and Kasich, each of whom provided vision and leadership, and
- The General Assembly, whose enabling legislation stands today.

This outstanding leadership has enabled frameworks and infrastructure focused on the Innovation Economy that are great assets, delivering strong benefits. Building out the capacity of these existing assets to connect to disconnected Ohioans, expanded to include women, is a policy that has significant merit.

Ohio taxpayers invest heavily in higher education research, commercialization, technology transfer, higher growth entrepreneurship, private capital formation, attraction and investment, and other forms of economic support. The state is counting on these investments to yield enterprises that create jobs in Ohio. It is not unreasonable to expect that beneficiaries of public support "pay forward" such support through participation in *Inclusive Competitiveness* efforts and activities, thereby helping disconnected Ohioans connect to and improve productivity and quality of life in the Innovation Economy.

UNANIMOUS ADOPTION

The final report of the subcommittee was unanimously adopted by the ODHE and reflected the priority of this area within Governor John Kasich's administration and within the University System of Ohio. It represents the first time stewards of a state university system have developed, adopted, and advocated a policy framework to improve the productivity of disconnected citizens in the twenty-first century Innovation Economy.

The report and recommendations are an initial step in creating and implementing an action blueprint. It details how Ohio's fourteen research universities, twenty-four regional branch campuses, and twenty-three community colleges can lead the way to dramatically improve access, opportunities, and outcomes for disconnected Ohioans within the state's myriad and diverse innovation and entrepreneurship ecosystems. The plan highlights that improved connectivity to and productivity within Ohio's emerging technology clusters, industry sectors, and other areas are critical to Ohio's sustained education and economic competitiveness.

After the release of the report on statewide *Inclusive Competitiveness*, a bright light shined on the activity and lack of progress on implementing Ohio law mandating outreach to disconnected Ohioans. Since then, the OTF Initiative has begun to move in a positive direction. Meaningful advancements worthy of note include:

- The $10 million fund dedicated solely to supporting female and minority entrepreneurs,
- An increased emphasis of the importance of inclusion through specific programming, promotional efforts, and criteria upon which funds are awarded to its innovation and entrepreneurship partners and grantees,
- An investment of $1 million to create an internship program dedicated to helping minority and rural students connect with early-stage ventures, and
- For the first time, tracking mechanisms employed to hold those grantees and partners accountable for their performance in the area of economic inclusion and competitiveness.[121]

These are early and promising developments which bode well for the future of economic inclusion and competitiveness in Ohio.

Commendable too is the recent success of the Ohio Minority Business Enterprise Program (MBE Program). Passed by Ohio Legis-

---

121 "Building a More Inclusive Entrepreneurial Ecosystem," National Venture Capital Association, July 2016, accessed November 30, 2016, http://nvca.org/ecosystem/diversity/.

lature in 1980, the program is designed to ensure that a minimum of 15 percent of government contracts are awarded to minority-owned businesses. Until recently, that goal had remained unmet for thirty-five consecutive years. Under Governor John Kasich's leadership however, in 2015, for the first time, Ohio awarded an impressive 19 percent of state contracts to minority-owned businesses and greatly surpassed the minimum specification.[122]

Unfortunately, while both the MBE Programs and the OTF Initiative are enshrined in state law, the latter's minority outreach provisions are now only beginning to receive significant attention from the State of Ohio. In fact, as discussed above, the MBE Program has no connectivity with the OTF Initiative. In the absence of any statewide strategy to improve productivity of disconnected Ohioans within the Innovation Economy, the progress being made, while impressive, is tempered. Thanks to the subcommittee, Ohio has an opportunity to change that.

The subcommittee has articulated the opening way forward to make Ohio *the* national model of twenty-first century education and economic inclusion and competitiveness. Certainly, any organization or government body interested in implementing and promoting *Inclusive Competitiveness* principles, policies, and actions would be wise to review and learn from what Ohio has done and is doing to meet these goals.

---

122 Hailey Wallace, "A Conversation With John Kasich," *Black Enterprise*, February 9, 2016, accessed November 30, 2016, http://www.blackenterprise.com/news/politics/a-conversation-with-john-kasich/2/.

CHAPTER 6

FROM TIP TO TRANSFORMATION

REVERSING TRENDS AND REVITALIZING COMMUNITIES IN THE INNOVATION ECONOMY

TIPPING POINTS

When a "star" is at the apex of his or her career, that person's popularity and success may appear larger than life. Consider celebrities like Erick Estrada, Anthony Michael Hall, Cyndi Lauper, Sinead O'Connor, Richard Simmons, and Jimmie Walker: at one time, these were the defining names and faces of their period, with millions of adoring fans and a run of musical, television, or cinematic hits. These personalities prove the rule that the fame doesn't last forever. Sometimes, legendary bands break up, celebrities make poor life and career choices, or public tastes simply change.

Similar phenomena occur in communities: cities like Cleveland, Detroit, Pittsburgh, and Chicago were global manufacturing powerhouses at one time. Unfortunately, they were unable to maintain those positions of leadership indefinitely. They approached the point of no return when too many forces conspired against these successful cities and tipped the balance in a negative direction. "Safe" areas became crime-ridden, bustling economic hubs of business activity dried up, and once-desirable neighborhoods declined into a collection of abandoned homes and run-down structures.

Malcolm Gladwell talks about this phenomenon in his book *The Tipping Point*, where he investigates "the moment of critical mass, the threshold, the boiling point"[123] for a community, organization, or even a fashion trend when a tendency or movement gains enough momentum that it becomes self-sustaining. Originally, this notion of a tipping point stemmed from early fair housing litigation and studies, from the late '60s and early '70s. Most recently, researchers Card, Mas, and Rothstein revisited that theme, discovering that a critical mass of minority residents often results in "White flight": this is where a once predominantly White neighborhood "tips" and begins to change into a minority one. In their study, they conclude that a "tipping point" is triggered and the White population exits when the locality's minority population approaches 5-20 percent.[124]

In terms of community economic development, I've adapted my concept of tipping points from that of Professors Henry Taylor and Sam Cole from the University at Buffalo. Their concepts are based on the idea that when people or a community on a regressive or downward

---

123 Malcolm Gladwell, *The tipping point: How little things can make a big difference*, (Boston: Little, Brown, 2000), p. 12.
124 David Card, Alexandre Mas, Jesse Rothstein, ., "Tipping and the Dynamics of Segregation," 2008, accessed September 26, 2015, http://www.nber.org/papers/w13052.

trajectory pass the tipping threshold, i.e., achieve critical mass, the forces of decline begin to greatly accelerate. We can envision this as an imaginary man—let's call him John Smith—who is running down a hill at full speed, accelerating with each step until he's out of control. With enough momentum, he might even catapult in the air, flying to the bottom of the hill, where he lands in a heap.

So too, struggling cities may reach a point of no return—where revitalization becomes extremely difficult, if not impossible. When communities tip, they experience population declines, job loss, decreased wealth, and a host of other negative consequences.

One of the clearest examples of a city reaching a tipping point is in Detroit. During my lifetime, Detroit has lost about 1.2 million people. Growing up, we took pride in our area's central city. It was the fifth largest in the U.S. with a population of just under two million and fell in just behind New York, Los Angeles, Chicago, and Philadelphia. Today, the city only has about 680,000 residents.[125]

That means that over the last forty years, Detroit has experienced a downward trajectory—with a dramatic decrease in manufacturing jobs, General Motors' bankruptcy, violent crimes, and extreme debt for the city—and has accelerated to the point where it is exceedingly difficult to reverse the trend. Today, property is dirt cheap and essentially gentrified, so investors are coming in to buy it up in hopes of a fresh start. However, turning the proverbial ship around is going to be quite a challenge. Who will lead the way? What kind of innovation can help Detroit? Can the city stop the downward spiral and reverse the trend in the opposite direction?

---

125 Detroit (city) QuickFacts from the U.S. Census Bureau, accessed September 26, 2015, http://quickfacts.census.gov/qfd/states/26/2622000.html.

TURNING POINTS

The idea of *turning point thresholds* from Professors Taylor and Cole explains how a community can begin to revitalize itself after its tip has commenced and stop itself from reaching the point of no return. This threshold "accelerates the developmental process, creating a snowballing effect"[126] that brings the community out of its slump. For this to occur, "fiscal investments ... must rise above a particular threshold ... [and this can be the result of money that is spent on] housing rehabilitation and construction, streets, sidewalks, curbs, landscaping, street-scaping, workforce development, and education."[127] In other words, incremental improvements in area conditions will not fundamentally change the community unless those "investments are sufficient to push ... beyond the *turning point threshold*."[128] Otherwise, the community will not be able to create enough momentum to initiate positive change.

Let's revisit our friend John Smith within the context of the turning point threshold: now instead of running downhill, he's running uphill. He gains momentum—he may slip and fall, but he doesn't quit. Rather, he gets up, dusts off, and influences and encourages others to run with him. Together they create uphill speed and synergy. Similarly, a set of positive multipliers can activate and turn a community in a positive direction.

However, it can be difficult to achieve the necessary uphill momentum to create a turning point. Here's why: when John Smith is running downhill, he's already got significant momentum. So, how could you stop him when he's running at full speed—and tipping with momentum? There is only one way: you'd have to gang tackle him.

---

126 Henry Louis Taylor, Jr. and Sam Cole, "Structural Racism and Efforts to Radically Reconstruct The Inner-City Built Environment," 2001, accessed September 26, 2015, http://www.thecyberhood.net/documents/papers/taylor01.pdf.
127 Ibid.
128 Ibid.

Sounds easy, but in the real world, rarely are we able to generate enough human and financial resources to intervene or "gang tackle" with the necessary scale and magnitude to stop or reverse the tip.

Initiating a turning point in this instance is extremely challenging, because the forces that drive these tips are huge. Despite their enormity, communities tend to treat them with glancing punches and never gather enough means, strategy, and leadership to truly intervene with a mighty blow that will halt the tip and begin the long, challenging journey toward the turn.

TRANSFORMATION POINTS IN THE INNOVATION ECONOMY

I have expanded the theories of Taylor and Cole by moving beyond turning points into the realm of *transformation*. As the professors indicate, to push traditional economic revitalization efforts in disconnected communities beyond that point requires more than a *new degree* of intervention, with positive multipliers set off by the magnitude of investments. Indeed, for transformation to occur, it is also necessary to introduce an entirely *new kind* of intervention that is aligned with the twenty-first century. And that is where the Innovation Economy calls for the transformative power of the *IC Framework*.

The key distinction between traditional community economic development in disconnected communities and *Inclusive Competitiveness* is this: the former lines up with the status quo and occurs within the proverbial "conventional zone," while the latter supports local economic competitiveness levers and occurs outside that conventional zone.

Although positive strides can be made in the "conventional zone," there is insufficient opportunity to achieve enough momentum to advance community economic development across the *transformation* threshold, resulting in the creation of something new (i.e., community transformation).

In iconoclastic fashion, *Inclusive Competitiveness* begins the process of breaking through traditional policies, strategies, and practices to create better ones that are more workable and productive in today's evolved economy. It embraces new approaches to help disconnected communities by preparing them to compete for our nation's best economic opportunities.

CONVENTIONAL ZONE AND TRANSFORMATION: AN ILLUSTRATION

The illustration on the next page further uses the metaphor of the different states of water to demonstrate the concept of transformation. The area in the center of the illustration represents the conventional zone. Water in this zone varies from cold (33 degrees Fahrenheit) to hot (211 degrees). Although there is a significant difference between the two temperatures, the water in this zone is just that: water. The base element does not change.

Now, when the temperature changes by just one degree in either direction out of the conventional zone the base element transforms. When one more degree of heat is applied to the water that is already at 211 degrees, it makes a clear change. It crosses a threshold to 212 degrees and becomes steam. It's no longer water, because it has been transformed.

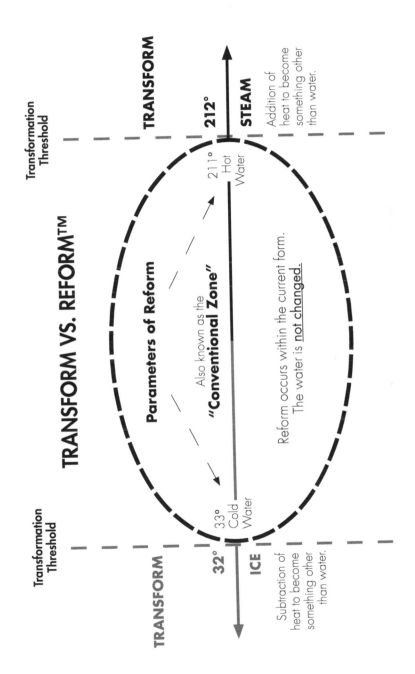

TRANSFORM VS. REFORM™

Transformation Threshold

TRANSFORM

212° **STEAM**

Addition of heat to become something other than water.

211° Hot Water

Parameters of Reform

Also known as the **"Conventional Zone"**

Reform occurs within the current form. The water is **not changed.**

33° Cold Water

Transformation Threshold

32° **ICE**

TRANSFORM

Subtraction of heat to become something other than water.

At the other end of the scale, when the temperature in the conventional zone is lowered just one more degree, crossing the other threshold, there is another change. Moving from 33 degrees to 32 degrees, the water freezes and begins its transformation into ice. However, until that threshold has passed, the water is not altered to a transformative degree.

A great deal of progress can be made within the 178-degree range (from 33 to 211 degrees) of the conventional zone. That change is called reform, and it can be a good thing! However, the status quo does not fundamentally change, since the base element remains the same.

Reform efforts can make a positive impact, yet they still do not sufficiently transform the community. Real transformation is when change happens beyond the conventional and the "water" (e.g., community investments, practices, programs, policies, etc.) changes into ice or steam.

In the same way, the *IC Framework* is designed to deliver change that goes beyond the incremental improvements of the status quo to create conditions for renewal within communities. If a community remains in the conventional zone, it will lack innovation, will not elicit real change, and will continue to be based on past practice and/or customary beliefs. On the other hand, *Inclusive Competitiveness* measures embrace the transformative change process through twenty-first century policies, strategies, practices, and programs.

The *IC Framework* is designed to provide disconnected communities with the tools they need to push progress out beyond the status quo (beyond convention) to create renewed, economically competitive communities.

In the case of Detroit, its bankruptcy may be enough to begin to lift the city out of the conventional zone. This historic event certainly set a new precedent for other troubled cities: they now know bankruptcy could also be an option (albeit painful) for them. For these tipped communities, the tumultuous intervention of municipal bankruptcy has the potential to provide them with an opportunity to jettison all manner of financial burdens and other legacy challenges and reverse the decline. These cities could very well maneuver themselves into a position where true transformation can occur. But without a major intervention—whether by bankruptcy or other means—a way out is not assured. Just as tipping points reach critical mass through accumulated difficulties over a period of time, points of transformation also need large amounts of momentum and power to reverse those negative trends.

WHO WILL LEAD THE CHARGE?

Let's look at another city: Cleveland, Ohio. Called one of the most innovative cities in America,[129] Cleveland is fortunate to be home to an extraordinary amount of twenty-first century economic assets. Among them are anchor institutions such as The Cleveland Clinic, University Hospitals of Cleveland, Case Western Reserve University, NASA John H. Glen Research Center, Cleveland State University, and the world's first community foundation, The Cleveland Foundation. These anchors support one of the Midwest's leading innovation and entrepreneurship ecosystems. It is comprised of venture development and business accelerator organizations, private investment capital, and key professional service providers. However, disconnected Clevelanders are mired in stunningly lower economic productivity levels. In fact, a recent study of 115 mid-sized U.S. metropolitan areas reveals just how serious the

---

129 Jillian Eugenios, Steve Hargreaves, and Aimee Rawlins, "Most Innovative Cities: The most innovative cities in America," *CNNMoney,* October 10, 2014, accessed November 30, 2016, http://money.cnn.com/gallery/technology/2014/10/07/most-innovative-cities/10.html.

situation is: the Cleveland Metro region ranks 94th for gross regional product, 91st for employment, and 88th for productivity.[130]

So then, how do Cleveland and the Northeast Ohio region capitalize on these assets and subsequently improve their economic performance? The city itself must first improve its economic performance. Then we also need to take a look at some demographics. Who comprises the population and is the economic foundation of the city? Interestingly, two-thirds of Cleveland's population is Black and Hispanic.

That means the city of Cleveland cannot improve its economic performance without Blacks and Hispanics improving their productivity; if the city of Cleveland doesn't improve, then it will place a dispro-portionate drag on the rest of the Northeast Ohio region, materially degrading its overall economic performance.

As indicated in earlier pages, these unrelenting demographic realities dictate who we are as a nation, and until we foster more productivity from these traditionally lower performing groups, we won't be able to optimally compete in the twenty-first century global economy. If, however, we begin to improve the productivity of disconnected populations, we position the nation for long-term economic prosperity. Improved economic productivity does not just spring up in communities out of nowhere. On the contrary, many communities are helped along by the power of regional innovation and entrepreneurship ecosystems that are nurtured by intermediary organizations.

---

130 Emily Garr Pacetti, "Building on Growth and Creating Opportunity: The Dual Imper-ative for Mid-Sized, U.S. Metros in the Recovery," What Matters to Metros™, Fund for Our Economic Future, October 1, 2013, accessed September 26, 2015, http://www.thefundneo.org/sites/default/files/content-media/13076_FUND_WMM_REVISED 1008.pdf.

INTERMEDIARY ORGANIZATIONS

The U.S. Small Business Administration defines intermediaries as "Organizations that play a fundamental role in encouraging, promoting, and facilitating business-to-business linkages and mentor-protégé partnerships. These can include both nonprofit and for-profit organizations: chambers of commerce; trade associations; local, civic, and community groups; state and local governments; academic institutions; and private corporations."[131] Again, it's all about facilitating and making connections. If intermediary organizations did not exist, then promising entrepreneurs and businesses would be surrounded by a community of lawyers, CPAs, investors, and other service providers—but they also would be without efficient and effective means by which to locate and engage these necessary resources.

Thought leaders on the subject of innovation-based economic development and competitiveness stress that "the innovation intermediary has two primary functions:

- The intermediary must provide operating mechanisms for regional connectivity, and
- It must serve as an accelerator which advances technologies and innovations into the marketplace for regional economic benefit."[132]

As discussed in Chapter 4, TTOs (Trim Tab Organizations) are intermediary organizations.

---

131 U.S. Small Business Administration, Office of Government Contracting | Resources, accessed September 26, 2015, https://www.sba.gov/offices/headquarters/ogc/resources/13275.

132 Richard A. Bendis, Richard S. Seline and Ethan J. Byler, "A new direction for technology-based economic development: The role of innovation intermediaries," Industry & Higher Education Vol 22, No 2, April 2008, p 76, accessed November 30, 2016, https://www.interdependence.org/wp-content/uploads/2011/11/s2_bendis-1.pdf.

In Cincinnati, for example, if you were an entrepreneur you would go to a place like CincyTech, an intermediary organization that creates connections and efficiencies within the regional economy for the entrepreneur. As the entrepreneur, you come in with a great idea, a lot of energy, some enthusiasm, and maybe a little money. At this point, CincyTech—the intermediary—uses its internal expertise and market relationships to create business development and growth opportunities. It links the entrepreneur to the kind of professional services that are needed and helps them prepare for potential investment in their enterprise.

As a result, the entrepreneur does not have to try to find all of the resources he or she may need. Instead, the intermediary is the connector between the entrepreneur and the world of services and the available human and financial resources.

In the case of CincyTech, I led approximately three hundred volunteer collaborators to create teams that would explore ways to accelerate tech-based development in Cincinnati.[133]

Cincinnati's leading corporations—such as Procter & Gamble, Macy's (known at the time as Federated Department Stores), The E.W. Scripps Company, and Cincinnati Bell—contributed to teams that encompassed several areas of regional technology and innovation advancement. These included: Startup Capital and Resources, High-Tech Image, Public Policy, and Research and Commercialization. From there, the teams made recommendations that would help accelerate the impact, growth, and sustainability tech-based innovation and entrepreneurship in the region.

---

133 Report of the Regional Technology Initiative, *Revving Up the Tech Engine: A Community Initiative to Drive Growth and Prosperity*, Greater Cincinnati Chamber of Commerce, 2001.

CincyTech is one of the Midwest's top intermediary venture development organizations. It is a credit to its team and the university, business, and nonprofit leadership in the Cincinnati region. I am proud to have led the effort that created it.

Innovation intermediary organizations are those in which talented and well-compensated professionals gather the necessary resources and connect the right people together to bring great ideas and business models to fruition. Essentially, they nurture, facilitate, and support ecosystems that consist of public and private capital, investors, research and development institutions, educational entities, workforce solutions providers, entrepreneurs, professional services, and governments. With intermediary organizations at the heart of the economic competitiveness network, a healthy ecosystem can grow and thrive in any given region. And while intermediary organizations lend themselves to the success of HGEs they can also positively affect the educational and workforce development systems, politics, policies, and small businesses in that city or region.

Cleveland's abundance of Innovation Economy assets is connected together by key intermediary organizations that support regional economic competitiveness. However, similar to nearly all other mid-sized and major cities in the U.S., there is an absence of intermediary organizations operating in and serving the disconnected communities in that region.

In and of themselves, effective economic development and competitiveness intermediary organizations (TTOs) do not create or grow companies and jobs. Rather, they lead the way to create a conducive *environment* in which these desired outcomes can occur. Moreover, disconnected communities do not require *lots* of intermediary organizations to take on the day-to-day work of aggregating, organizing, and leveraging business and entrepreneurship development, workforce solutions, and social, educational, and human services. In fact, communities need just one or two effective organizations to catalyze, lead, and sustain processes that promote transformation. Positions in these organizations are by no means secondary low-paying roles: they are vital to effecting change and need to be well-compensated day jobs.

LEVERAGING THE CHARITABLE PURPOSE

More than a dozen years ago, I was vice chairman of The Greater Cincinnati Foundation (one of the nation's largest community foundations with net assets of $542 million)[134] and chairman of the Economic Development Task Force. These were the early days of the philanthropic community across the U.S. beginning to discover both its general role in economic development and its specific role in tech- and innovation-based activities.

Today, the philanthropic sector has taken an active role in supporting nonprofit intermediary organizations focused on economic development and competitiveness.[135] Over the past generation, these nonprofit organizations have proliferated throughout the nation. They are running venture capital funds, recruiting companies to major metropolitan areas, providing technical assistance to business owners, and in a multitude of other ways facilitating economic growth in urban, suburban, and rural areas throughout the country.[136] According to Case Western Reserve University law professor Matthew Rossman, all fifty major metropolitan areas in the U.S. have a nonprofit organization

---

134 "About GCF," The Greater Cincinnati Foundation, accessed November 30, 2016, https://www.gcfdn.org/portals/0/uploads/documents/about_gcf.pdf.
135 Ibid.
136 Matthew J. Rossman, "Evaluating Trickle Down Charity – A Solution for Determining When Economic Development Aimed at Revitalizing America's Cities and Regions is Really Charitable," Case Research Paper Series in Legal Studies Working Paper 2014-01, January 2014, accessed November 30, 2016, p. 3, http://ssrn.com/abstract=2376470.

with a primary mission of regional job creation.[137] The majority of these organizations were created in the past sixteen years.[138]

Many communities are harnessing the power of nonprofit intermediaries. They use them to create efficiencies in an otherwise unwieldy system of city, regional, and state economic development and competitiveness, connecting assets, services, and resources over and over again.

Many of these nonprofit intermediaries also happen to be charities or 501(c)(3) organizations. These organizations have distinct advantages over for-profit and other nonprofit organizations, as they are:

- Exempt from federal income tax (and, by extension, from many other types of federal, state, and local taxes),
- Eligible for contributions that are tax-deductible by individual and corporate donors from their federal income tax,
- Eligible for funding from government and foundation sources that are either not available to or harder to obtain for non-501(c)(3) organizations, and
- Conferred public credibility associated with having been scrutinized by the IRS and recognized as a charity.[139]

Taken together, these advantages amount to a substantial public subsidy intended to offer an incentive to the philanthropic work of private organizations,[140] which makes the 501(c)(3) designation very attractive to economic development and competitiveness organizations.

There is an important caveat when considering the positive impact that a 501(c)(3) nonprofit intermediary can make: *the organization must be committed to fulfilling its charitable purpose.* While this may appear

---

137 Ibid.
138 Ibid.
139 Ibid, p. 4.
140 Ibid.

to be a "no-brainer," it is an unfortunate reality that many economic development and competitiveness charities may not be as charitable as we think.

The term "charitable," as used in Internal Revenue Code, is defined to mean the "promotion of social welfare by organizations designed to accomplish" any of the following purposes:

- Relief of the poor and distressed or of the underprivileged,
- Lessening of the burdens of government,
- Lessening neighborhood tensions,
- Elimination of prejudice and discrimination,
- Defense of human and civil rights secured by law, and
- Combatting community deterioration and juvenile delinquency.

To receive this public subsidy, a group must be organized and operated *exclusively for charitable purposes.* They must serve "public" and not "private" interests. In other words, the primary and direct beneficiaries of the 501(c)(3) nonprofit intermediary must be the members of a charitable class; any resulting benefit to private interests must be an incidental and insignificant byproduct of serving the charitable class.[141] In my experience, the connection of many economic development and competitiveness charities to the charitable class, or disconnected people and communities, is at best, attenuated and at worst, nonexistent.

TROUBLING EXPERIENCE AND OBSERVATIONS

As described earlier in this chapter, I have worked on this matter with a leading philanthropic organization, The Greater Cincinnati Foundation.

---

141 Ibid, p. 5.

Our objective was to consider the best way to be active in, and positively impact, economic development and competitiveness, and at the same time ensure that the charitable purpose is fulfilled.

Informed by this background, over the past ten years or so, I have had difficult experiences with leaders of local innovation and entrepreneurship ecosystems when it comes to the intersection of philanthropy and economic development. Despite hundreds of millions of dollars invested in economic development and competitiveness by philanthropy throughout the U.S. there is scarcely an identifiable strategy aligned with twenty-first century imperatives to improve the situation of disconnected communities and populations. Nor is there a meaningful difference in their productivity and competitiveness.

It is important to note that economic development and competitiveness are not in and of themselves charitable. What makes these activities charitable largely depends on where and for whom they are carried out. Charitable dollars that support economic development and competitiveness should be primarily invested in, and be used expressly for the benefit of targeted distressed communities and underserved populations. Yet, it is highly questionable whether these groups and areas are generally the direct beneficiaries of those dollars.

Philanthropic funders need a firm and continuous effort to demand economic inclusion and competitiveness. Their leadership and investment in innovation and entrepreneurship ecosystems should ensure that meaningful financial and human resources are deployed where they are needed to advance disconnected communities. This will safeguard against resources being drawn away from the charitable class for the sole benefit of private interests such as non-charitable class, higher growth entrepreneurship, investors, researchers, and service providers. From my experience with economic development and competitiveness charities, many may have turned upside-down the spirit of 501(c)(3) status wherein the "primary and direct beneficiaries" may be the non-charitable class and any resulting benefit to the charitable class is the "incidental and insignificant byproduct of serving" non-charitable interests.

INTERESTING INTERSECTIONS WITH NATURE

Over the past decade, I have noticed an increased interest from corporate and philanthropic funders to explore ways to enable and support various kinds of systems (social, education, and economic) to facilitate more impactful community leadership and outcomes. However, such promising talk has yet to manifest in meaningful investments in revitalization systems in disconnected communities. While there is a desire for systems, what is still lacking is a willingness to invest in the kind of structures that can catalyze, build, and sustain those systems.

Instead, what I am seeing is that direct-service providers in disconnected communities are fiercely competing against one another to survive. The capacity for innovation and productivity growth is severely limited by the predominant organizational model in these areas. That model is comprised of a proliferation of low-barrier to entry and low-differentiation services. Unfortunately, innovative solutions are unlikely with the current structures that are in place.[142]

"An approach to innovation that seeks sustainable solutions to human challenges by emulating nature's time-tested patterns and strategies,"[143] is called *biomimicry*, i.e., mimicking biology. Perhaps not

---

142 Marco Iansiti and Roy Levien, , "Keystones and Dominators: Framing Operating and Technology Strategy in a Business Ecosystem," Ferbruary 24, 2004, accessed September 26, 2015, p. 25, http://www.keystonestrategy.com/wp-content/themes/keystone-theme/publications/pdf/Ecosystems.pdf.

143 "What Is Biomimicry?" Biomimicry Institute, 2015, accessed September 26, 2015, http://biomimicry.org/what-is-biomimicry/#.VfXSgkDXHRg.

surprisingly, there are definite parallels with the natural world with respect to the economy and community organizations and systems.

For example, it is estimated that by 2050, the world will have to roughly double the number of crops it grows[144] and do that from farm acreage similar to that which we cultivate today. The U.S. economy faces a similar challenge, to increase jobs and prosperity from our existing population. Agriculture's successful approach to boosting farm yields from existing acreage can inform our efforts to grow jobs and prosperity largely from our existing population. Their answer is biodiversity.

Biodiversity refers to the variety of plants, animals, and microorganisms above and below the soil that interact within an ecosystem.[145] Researchers have found overwhelming evidence that the net effect of having fewer species in an ecosystem is a reduced quantity of plant biomass.[146] In fact, ecosystems containing several different species are more productive than individual species on their own.[147] The upshot is that biodiversity is essential to meeting the world's food production needs. And, in the same way, economic inclusion and competitiveness are essential to meeting our nation's job and enterprise creation needs and aspirations for sustained prosperity in the modern world.

Furthermore, in nature, there is a particular type of species referred to as a "keystone." It has "a disproportionate effect on other organisms within the system" because its "impact on the community

---

144 Jonathon Foley, "A Five-Step Plan to Feed the World, The Future of Food," *National Geographic Magazine*, accessed November 30, 2016, http://www.nationalgeographic.com/foodfeatures/feeding-9-billion/.

145 Annette Wszelaki, Associate Professor and Commercial Vegetable Extension Specialist, Sarah Broughton, Former Graduate Research Assistant Department of Plant Sciences, "Increasing Farm Biodiversity," University of Tennessee Institute for Agriculture, accessed November 30, 2016, https://extension.tennessee.edu/publications/Documents/W235-D.pdf.

146 Anita Fors, "Biodiversity leads to higher productivity," University of Gothenburg, Science Daily, March 22, 2011, accessed November 30, 2016, https://www.sciencedaily.com/releases/2011/03/110321183015.htm.

147 Ibid.

is greater than would be expected based on its relative abundance or total biomass."[148] In other words, a keystone species can have an *exponential* impact on other organisms, even though its size might be perceived as "small." Likewise, intermediary organizations (TTOs) can help deliver great change and success for a community. Oftentimes it does not take a massive conglomerate to do so. Instead, it is the purposeful actions of intermediary organizations that can help drive a region into unprecedented success (and those intermediaries do not need to be large).

Modern forward-thinking leaders are embracing this philosophy in building their organizations. In an interview with BBC News, John Mackey, chief executive at supermarket chain Whole Foods, says: "We need leaders who have a higher degree of systems intelligence that can see how it all fits together and that understand the importance of creating value for all of these stakeholders. It's a different kind of leader to who we typically have."[149]

Almost all evolved networks of interacting elements have their stability and function governed by keystones, hubs, or some form of centralized or shared control.[150] The TTO is the keystone that loosely governs efforts to connect disconnected people and communities to regional innovation and entrepreneurship ecosystems, providing both centralized and shared leadership.

---

148 Iansiti, M., and Levien, R., "Keystones and Dominators: Framing Operating and Technology Strategy in a Business Ecosystem," February 24, 2004, accessed September 26, 2015, p. 26, http://www.keystonestrategy.com/wp-content/themes/keystone-theme/publications/pdf/Ecosystems.pdf.
149 http://www.bbc.com/news/business-33306101.
150 Iansiti, M., and Levien, R., "Keystones and Dominators: Framing Operating and Technology Strategy in a Business Ecosystem," February 24, 2004, accessed September 26, 2015, p. 25, http://www.keystonestrategy.com/wp-content/themes/keystone-theme/publications/pdf/Ecosystems.pdf.

LESSONS FROM ATHLETICS

To develop and implement programs with impact, projects, and initiatives, keystone organizations must provide effective, on-the-ground leadership. Consider it as leadership that is closest to the challenges experienced by disconnected communities. It links people and resources together.

This sports metaphor, lifted from my time as an athlete, is particularly pertinent. During my college and professional football career, I sustained several injuries that prevented me from performing at peak levels. These debilitating injuries usually involved my connective ligaments—the strong, slightly elastic, individual bands of tissue that connect bone to bone. I did, however, have good bones and rarely were they injured.

Regardless of bone strength, no athlete can perform at his or her highest capacity with injuries to their bone-connectors. Without exception, ligament damage will always downgrade performance. A community can be likened to a great athlete with good, strong bones. The community's bones are the resilient and talented people. They are the robust art, culture, business, religion, philanthropy, education, government, economic development, and human service institutions. And damaged or non-existent connections within communities will always prevent them from achieving peak performance.

Most communities rarely experience a breakdown in their people and institutions (their "bones"). Rather, they sustain severe damage to their connective "ligaments," the very elements that bind them together. To overcome the pressing challenges facing disconnected communities, and begin to halt and turn around the tip, the keystone organizations (TTOs) must be the "ligaments" that connect community "bones. They must connect twenty-first century opportunities to disconnected people and their institutions.

It is essential to underpin communities with strong TTO keystones that help build new capacities and capabilities. Systems development in disconnected communities that fail to include TTOs as keystones are essentially attempting to defy the laws of nature. We cannot expect systems thinking, planning, leadership, and action to emerge without investing in those intermediary organizations and functions that can bring them about. Exercising the connections ("ligaments" to "bones") will increase overall community ("body") strength by creating a solid, enabling foundation from which to work.

Sometimes people think intermediary organizations need to be some sort of mega-organization, however that is far from the truth. These organizations do not have to be huge, nor are many needed. A community needs just one to a small number of good quality hubs. That's because the systems-based, relational nature of intermediary organizations is what makes the difference. Remember, a trim tab is small—even though it helps steer a big ship—and an intermediary is no different. TTOs can exert an impact on the community that is many times greater than what one may expect based on relative size. The crucial metric of an intermediary organization is the ratio of size-to-mission impact.

A wonderful example of an effective keystone intermediary organization resides in St. Louis. BioSTL is a relatively small organization of approximately ten employees and has an annual budget of about $7 million.[151] It is the TTO for biosciences growth and development in the St. Louis region. This community-connector advances economic vitality: it cultivates a strong bioscience innovation and entrepreneurship ecosystem, and organizes business, university, and philanthropic

---

151 Brian Feldt, "BioSTL wins $500,000 federal grant to create accelerator programs," *St. Louis Business Journal*, March 31, 2015, accessed November 30, 2016, http://www. bizjournals.com/stlouis/blog/biznext/2015/03/biostl-wins-500-000-federal-grant-to-create.html.

leaders all around a set of deliberate strategies that capitalize on St. Louis' strengths in medical and plant sciences.[152] BioSTL recognizes that creating jobs and economic prosperity for a region is a complex undertaking requiring broad collaboration. It leverages its efforts by devoting human and financial resources to shared needs such as marketing, data collection, and training entrepreneurs. By assisting its partners, it relieves those individual organizations from the need to divert resources away from their core missions. In this way, BioSTL promotes the efficient use of limited regional resources.[153] Significantly, BioSTL is an early adopter of *Inclusive Competitiveness* concepts.[154]

BioSTL's many successes include building and investing in startup companies through its subsidiary, BioGenerator. A venture development organization, BioGenerator improves access to investment capital, ensures appropriate physical infrastructure, promotes science- and innovation-friendly public policy, fosters a more inclusive entrepreneurial talent pool in the region, attracts the U.S. presence of international companies, and widely communicates St. Louis' strengths. BioGenerator has been investing funds since 2004.[155] A total of $10.3 million has been meaningfully leveraged nineteen to one: this translates to $195.6 million in investment capital, grants, and revenue that has been raised by their portfolio companies.[156]

TTOs clearly can make a difference. They are an economic keystone species of the Innovation Economy and can have a huge impact. Through

---

152 "BioSTL," accessed November 30, 2016, www.biostl.org.

153 Ibid.

154 Mary Mack, "Getting Everyone Involved: How BioSTL And Dr. Cheryl Watkins-Moore Are Bringing New Talent To The Life Sciences Sector," *EQ*, September 19, 2016, accessed November 30, 2016, http://eqstl.com/getting-everyone-involved-biostl-dr-cheryl-watkins-moore-bringing-new-talent-life-sciences-sector/.

155 " BioGenerator Mission and History," accessed November 30, 2016, http://biogenerator.org/about/our-mission/.

156 " BioGenerator Annual Report 2014," accessed November 30, 2016, http://www.biogenerator.org/wp-content/uploads/2015/07/BIOGENERATOR-ANNUAL-RE-PORT-2014.pdf.

their systems-driven approaches and purposeful actions they establish crucial connections and relationships. Not only can they help revitalize sagging disconnected communities, but also infuse new growth into regional economies, leading to sustainable success for far more people.

But ... where are these seemingly elusive TTOs to be found?

IN SEARCH OF TTOs

The popular children's book series *Where's Waldo?* challenges the reader to view a page with thousands of small illustrations in a quest to find the main character. But because there are so many other distractions on the page, it can be difficult to locate him. In the same way, TTOs do exist, but not everyone can see them or find them amidst all the other social, education, and economic organizations, programs, and initiatives. However, in disconnected communities throughout the country, TTOs, by and large, do not even exist.

TTOs can mostly be found on the economic development and competitiveness side of local organizations. Leaders in this space recognize that igniting economic progress involves *process* (a concept broached in Chapter 8 of this book). They know that someone needs to go to Washington, D.C., to bring resources back for economic development. They recognize that someone needs to aggregate, organize, and leverage local assets to create new opportunities. And they understand these tasks cannot be "extra" job responsibilities piled on top of individuals who are better suited for (and need to focus on) other aspects of an organization. Governments and foundations are simply not geared to do all of that work. If they cannot do it, then the work does not get done. At that point, we are all just out there, proverbially spinning our wheels, searching for ways to have a positive impact in the community without an efficient way to pursue those objectives. TTOs, on the other hand, provide the needed efficiency to streamline otherwise unwieldy local and regional environments.

It is the people in a TTO who help build and nurture an environment that is conducive to job, enterprise, and wealth creation. In this way TTOs provide stewardship to the local or regional economy. They are proficient at identifying and filling gaps, bringing back resources from Washington, D.C. or state capitals, lobbying public officials to develop new sources of investment capital and other resources, and facilitating needed community connections. But the problem still remains: for disconnected communities, TTOs do not typically exist. Disconnected communities are rife with content-focused organizations, which deliver direct services without complementary, higher leverage, and more efficient process-oriented systems.

In disconnected communities, nearly all resources go to solely delivering value to the individual. And while this is necessary, these discrete efforts serve to overshadow the merit and necessity of intermediary organizations that help create new conditions to benefit the wider community. A paradox exists; while intermediaries act as the force multiplier, leading the process of connecting, fostering, and bringing together disparate resources and services for *exponential* impact, this can be difficult to measure. In contrast, direct-service organizations offer tangible and easily identifiable services that deliver only *singular* (individualized) impact.

To be sure, disconnected populations need organized assistance to find their "Waldo" and demand his help to aggregate and leverage the vital resources and build the systems needed to turn around their struggling communities!

The questions remain:

- How do we infuse disconnected communities with these vital TTOs?
- How do we equip and empower individuals to demand that new community systems of both direct-service providers *and* intermediary organizations become integral parts of their leadership and services infrastructure?
- What are the leadership principles that can inform initiation of a grassroots movement around economic inclusion and competitiveness?
- And, how do we educate and inspire disconnected populations to not just invite these new approaches and organizations into their communities ... but to *become* those approaches and organizations, for they themselves to *become* the transformative leaders of tomorrow?

The answer: by following 10 Leadership Principles to Advance *Inclusive Competitiveness*, which will be discussed in the next chapter.

CHAPTER 7

10 LEADERSHIP PRINCIPLES

TO ADVANCE INCLUSIVE COMPETITIVENESS

I t could be said that I have had an uncommon career because I have chosen a less travelled road. Mine was not a likely path: from captain of a winless high school football team, to walk-on athlete at a major college, to earning a scholarship, to being elected both a university student leader and football team captain, to the NFL and the Super Bowl, to civil rights lawyer, to a leader of historic and venerable community organizations, to a leader of innovation and economic competitiveness organizations.

What ties together these experiences is the good fortune of being afforded opportunities to grow into leadership roles at almost every step along the way. I've learned lots of individual, organizational, and community leadership lessons codified into enduring principles. I share these principles—gleaned from this deep and wide-ranging diversity of experiences—as I am confident they will provide communities and leaders with insights and context about how to successfully implement the *IC Framework*.

Importantly, these values are consistent with the principles and objectives of Asset Based Community Development (ABCD):[157] a groundbreaking strategy for sustainable community-driven development that goes beyond mere mobilization to link often unrecognized assets to the local economic opportunities.[158] The ABCD approach catalyzes change and development based on using the existing gifts and capacities of people and their communities.[159] However, while some forms of ABCD discourage development brought in from outside sources,[160] *Inclusive Competitiveness* encourages the attraction of new, outside Innovation Economy resources and the opportunities that attach to them. The critical alignment of ABCD and *Inclusive Competitiveness* is that both approaches are designed to energize change and development from within communities: the prime focus is on strengths, gifts, capacities, and finding areas where local assets meet needs rather than looking solely at community deficits.[161]

Although each one of the 10 Leadership Principles is not necessarily singularly remarkable, when you put them together, their synergy creates a powerful force. They are the behaviors that can enable the realization of *Inclusive Competitiveness.*

---

157 "What is Asset Based Community Development," Asset Based Community Development Institute, accessed November 30, 2016, http://www.abcdinstitute.org/docs/What%20isAssetBasedCommunityDevelopment(1).pdf.
158 Ibid.
159 "Asset-Based Community Development," Episcopal Relief & Development, accessed November 30, 2016, http://www.episcopalrelief.org/what-we-do/asset-based-community-development.
160 Ibid.
161 Ibid.

PRINCIPLE 1: SIMPLE OVER COMPLEX

In Chapter 4, I discussed the book *Good to Great* by Jim Collins, who suggests that organizations are basically either "complex" or "simple." I believe the same is true for leadership. Complex leadership has intricate, often convoluted plans, and involves pursuing many goals at the same time. Because its efforts are scattered, complex leadership seldom agrees on a vision and process that binds together and guides all their work.

On the other hand, simple leadership creates a true, clear picture of reality and knows how it fits within that reality. Simple leadership is aligned in thought and action. It is based on distilled principles that inform all activity and has a shared understanding of the work to be accomplished.

Inclusive Competitiveness leadership should be simple.

Collins' theory made quite an impression on me. In particular, what resonates is breaking down the complex into simple ideas. In 2000, I codified a simple, three-step process for community leaders that provides a straightforward approach to bring clarity to scary, unwieldy problems and can be undertaken with plain old hard work.

I call it the "A.O.L. process" (not to be confused with the global mass media company):

- **A**ggregate,
- **O**rganize, and
- **L**everage.

The beauty of this process is that it works for just about everything! No matter what the issue, these three steps can help you plan your response.

First, *Aggregate* your key assets. Determine whose help and what resources you need—money, talent, materials ... whatever. Then, bring these people and things together; convene them.

Next, *Organize* the aggregated assets. Together, explore ways to combine into an actionable form—a structured leadership team, a loose collaborative, an orderly network—that will labor together to get the team's desired result. An important point is that if you've aggregated the right resources, then they will largely self-organize. Your role is to provide them an opportunity and platform to do so.

And then, *Leverage* those key assets you've aggregated and organized. Find ways for them to discover their collective strength and how to overcome their weaknesses to achieve the desired result.

That is what it takes.

Here is an example of how A.O.L. works.

There were no technology-based schools in Ohio. Along with several other technology and innovation advocates, I wanted to make sure we were growing an inclusive innovation-based economy. We believed that creating the state's first technology-focused high school would help do that.

Our goal was to provide a unique educational experience that was not available in other area schools. Moreover, we felt that a new technology school would help establish our city—Cincinnati—as a national pioneer in urban education.

We used the A.O.L. model:

- *We determined the assets that needed to be* Aggregated. We connected the local chamber of commerce, the area's leading telecommunications company, the city school district, and a few thought-leading consultants.

- *Then, we decided how to* Organize *these Aggregated key assets.* We met with the key people, facilitated their alignment and commitment to the vision for a technology school, and we organized them into a work team.
- *Finally, we* Leveraged *the Aggregated and Organized assets.* Through the work team, our assets contributed meaningful resources—organizational and corporate staff, financial support, and thought leadership—that we used to create Robert A. Taft Information Technology High School. This became the first technology high school in Ohio and a national model of turn-around urban education.

Upshot: Keep it Simple

The A.O.L. approach is simple. It is a fundamental way of structuring your thinking, strategies, and actions. It is a reliable process that can be applied over and over again. In fact, the more you A.O.L. the better and more efficient you will become at it. However, simple does not necessarily mean easy. A lot of work goes into A.O.L. When approached correctly, this basic model can help *Inclusive Competitiveness* leadership position itself to best help disconnected communities work together to overcome challenges, take advantage of opportunities, and improve their economic productivity and quality of life.

PRINCIPLE 2: POISE OVER BLUSTER

It bears stating, even if this notion is largely understood: the best leadership tends to be confident and poised, rather than comprised of harangues of verbose and unwieldy statements. Grand declarations of instant (or magical) economic transformation of disconnected communities are not required for *Inclusive Competitiveness*. Rather, leaders are more like good quarterbacks on football teams. Quarterbacks are generally recognized as team leaders because of the nature of their job on the field. The best ones are not—and do not need to be—chest-thumpers. When it comes to *Inclusive Competitiveness* leadership, the motto could read: "Be the leader—no declaration needed."

For a few years, I was a teammate of former NFL quarterback Boomer Esiason of the Cincinnati Bengals. In the time I spent with the Bengals (and with Boomer personally), I don't ever recall hearing him boasting or "declaring" himself the leader. Boomer's demeanor was the "swagger of leadership." It inspired confidence and attracted followers. It was neither offensive nor repulsive. The whole team respected Boomer—who led us to the Super Bowl—and his leadership flowed from that respect. His leadership was derived by the consent of those he led.

Not all quarterbacks are as poised as Boomer was. The leader I knew was a self-assured, generous, and thoughtful man who passed on opportunities to his teammates so they too could stand in the spotlight. He never acted like an untouchable superstar. There was no bluster, and no attention-grabbing announcement of "Hey, I'm in charge" was needed. He simply and fully stepped into the role and fulfilled all his responsibilities by earning the trust and inspiring the confidence of his colleagues.

Upshot: Demonstrate Leadership Poise

Just as quarterbacks earn a level of trust and respect among their teammates, *Inclusive Competitiveness* leadership should be self-assured, inspire confidence, and create that same level of trust and respect within disconnected communities. To be successful, it can never lose sight of the reality that it can effectively lead only with the consent of the community. There's no doubt that remaining poised in what can be the white-hot fires of disconnected community leadership is tough. It's not easy to do what good quarterbacks do: they stand upright, offer reliable, sturdy support that delivers results, despite the relentless pass rushers surrounding them.

PRINCIPLE 3: RISK-ASTUTE OVER RISK-AVERSE

Risks are a part of every facet of life: we can either choose to take or avoid them. *Inclusive Competitiveness* leadership focuses on taking smart risks, or being *risk-astute*—rather than avoiding them altogether—or being *risk-averse*.

Inclusive Competitiveness requires taking smart risks and a willingness to take a chance on failure. Perhaps more important is the ability to accept the responsibilities that success brings, including heightened expectations to deliver even more success. Risk-astuteness involves assessing risk with both your *head* and *heart,* then moving forward—and that's the key, *moving forward.*

As I shared earlier, when I was a high school senior, our football team had a perfect season. *We lost every single game!* Not surprisingly, none of the big schools in my home state of Michigan recruited me. I asked Al Wilkerson, my basketball and track coach, to send game film to West Virginia University: I was invited to try out for the football team as a walk-on, with no scholarship and no guarantee. Sight-unseen, but informed by all my previous experiences, aspirations, and calculations, I decided to go to WVU.

At the Greyhound Bus Station in Detroit, my mother said, "Johnny, I want to get you a roundtrip ticket in case it doesn't work out." Although she was expressing deep love, her thinking was risk-averse. She was saying, "Here's a safety net if you fail." But I was eighteen and determined. Playing college football at a major university had been my dream since I was eight years old.

I had invested years of preparation for this opportunity. I had thought it through. I was all-in. So I said to my mother, "I'll take the one-way ticket. I'm not coming back home until I'm supposed to." Unbeknownst to me, at that moment, I confirmed my entrepreneurial bona fides. Adapting Harvard Business School Professor Howard Stevenson's definition of entrepreneurship—I pursued the opportunity to play major college football without regard to the resources that I controlled.

This wasn't crazy, risky behavior. There was no one in the world better informed and positioned to make this decision. For ten years, I had done the homework. I had watched guys from other schools earn athletic scholarships and perform at the highest level. I had assessed my talent and abilities against the players who had achieved what I wanted to achieve. I had deeply considered my possibilities of playing high-level college football and I believed that I had a real chance to make the team and earn a scholarship. So I took that one-way ticket.

I did well during spring workouts, and I caught the eye of the coaches on the scout team and in spring scrimmages. The next fall, I earned a full athletic scholarship. The following year, I earned a starting role and, in my senior year, my teammates elected me captain.

Just as successful *Inclusive Competitiveness* leadership does with disconnected communities, I had performed a similar internal process, making a clear assessment of my talent, abilities, the challenges ahead of me, and chances of achieving my objective. I put in all the hard work demanded of that desired achievement. There was no other way to get there. Then, I was prepared to go all-in, laying my chips on the table. And it paid off.

Upshot: Take Smart Risks

Inclusive Competitiveness leadership must take risks but it should never risk foolishly. Decisions and actions supporting *Inclusive Competitiveness* need to be made with thought and all the wisdom that can be mustered. Leadership should guide community processes–to assess talent, challenges, opportunities, and chances of improving productivity and quality of life for disconnected Americans in the Innovation Economy–then go all-in to achieve goals.

PRINCIPLE 4: POTENTIAL OVER ACTUAL

Actuality and potentiality leadership are as different as day and night. Actuality leaders perceive *limited* possibilities informed by what is already happening. Potentiality leaders perceive *unlimited* possibilities that have yet to be realized.

To paraphrase the playwright George Bernard Shaw, actuality leadership sees things as they are and asks "Why?" Potentiality leadership dreams things that never were and asks "Why not?" This mindset welcomes a future of endless possibilities. It knows, with complete faith and clarity, that every situation can be changed. On the other hand, actuality leaders see the future as just more of today ... with some progress, but no real change.

Too often, I've experienced disconnected community economic leadership that has fostered a culture of predetermined, existing, and limited opportunities, without spontaneous, future-oriented, and alterable possibilities. *Inclusive Competitiveness* leadership is that of potentiality motivated by the unlimited promise of untapped potential.

In Chapter 2, I described my relationship with a remarkable man, Dr. Milton Hinton. He was a potentiality leader and inspired others to be the same. I experienced this firsthand when I was a volunteer for the NAACP, working with the City of Cincinnati on ways to improve police-community relations. At a meeting where Dr. Hinton was presiding, someone said something I strongly disagreed with, and I pounded the table and said some pretty nasty words. I immediately regretted my crude, immature behavior—especially in front of this man I respected so much. But the dignified Dr. Hinton didn't even blink. If he'd been a person who only saw the actual, he would have taken me off his list of "reliable guys" right then and there.

But he didn't. He was looking for potential, and he saw that in me somewhere. He knew where my heart was and that I had a passion for making a difference—but I needed to grow up. He sensed my true regret and for that reason he knew that he didn't have to say a word.

Dr. Hinton continued to give me important assignments that made significant differences and that helped me to grow. He knew that I needed experience to become a mature advocate and activist. He had confidence in me and showed that he was committed to helping me fulfill my leadership potential.

Upshot: Explore Potential

If this mentor hadn't seen potential, my experiences would have been awfully different! Dr. Hinton did not "block" for me, proverbially cutting a clear path as I ran the football. No, his mentorship role was instrumental because he helped me *through* the growth and development process. To fulfil a community's potential, *Inclusive Competitiveness* does not miraculously take away the real struggles that they encounter. Focusing on potential is not a way to avoid the learning curve. It does, however, help the existing and emerging community leaders and organizations make sense of today's economy and coach them *through* the challenges and barriers. In this way, *Inclusive Competitiveness* leadership can help disconnected communities and their leaders grow from their current economic state to awaken largely dormant potential.

PRINCIPLE 5: ENTREPRENEURSHIP OVER ENTITLEMENT

Disconnected communities need change that transforms. The only way to reach this level of impact is through *entrepreneurial* leadership.

Entrepreneurship is a way of thinking. Consider new business and social enterprises as just two manifestations of such a mindset. Similarly, *entrepreneurial* leadership is a way of thinking that encourages us to go after opportunities on our own, beyond the capacity of our existing assets, rather than waiting for good things to happen for us. Entrepreneurs of all stripes are not constrained by the limitations of their own resources.

Entitled leadership operates from a foundation whereby opportunities—social, economic, education, and everything else—should be granted to it, as if dropped from above like heavenly manna. It feels that society, and particularly its own disconnected communities, is forever in its debt.

Inclusive Competitiveness leadership should reject the limiting and destructive notions of entitled thinking. Instead opportunities must be created, earned, and seized, and the only thing society owes is a fair chance for us to do our best. Just as entrepreneurs in the business world are, *Inclusive Competitiveness* leadership should be self-activated and self-motivated toward solutions.

Several years ago, I was a co-founder of Build Cincinnati, a team working for historic government reform in the city. Before the effort started, civic organizations and all three political parties in Cincinnati had tried for twenty years to make reforms without much success. We were the core of a new effort—the young guns, eager to change things. We met with the sitting Black city council members to tell them of our plans for changes we believed were in the best interest of the city.

During those meetings, we received assurances of support from these elected officials.

Confident of their backing, we launched the reform effort but were greatly surprised when those leaders not only showed no sign of support, they outright opposed us! One of their tenuous and manufactured objections was their claim that no Black candidate could ever be elected mayor of the city under our proposed new system.

Beneath it all was their belief that, as elected leaders, *they were entitled* to lead any government reform effort. We, on the other hand, did not ask for permission to lead. We were leading as civic entrepreneurs.

We felt sure of the homework we had done. We had the local and national election facts on our side, and in some cases these had been established in a court of law. We ignored their petty politics and won the day at the ballot box. For the record, in just the second election under the new system, the city elected a Black mayor for the first time in history. He served two terms in office.

Upshot: Think and Act Like an Entrepreneur

Inclusive Competitiveness leadership respects incumbent leaders in disconnected communities and always seeks to work with them, building bridges whenever possible. However, if those leaders' actions reflect entitlement thinking, then *Inclusive Competitiveness* leaders should meet that entitlement with the blunt force of entrepreneurship. They must vigorously pursue their goals and objectives and overcome the obstacles incumbent or entitled leaders may place in front of them. In sum, *Inclusive Competitiveness* leaders must never succumb to any temptation to mistake the awesome privilege of leadership for an entitled right to lead.

PRINCIPLE 6: INFLUENCE OVER COERCION

Robert K. Greenleaf, founder of the modern "servant leadership" movement, wrote: "Leadership rests mostly on persuasion and the responses to it are voluntary, not coerced."[162]

In other words, the highest form of leadership is about inspiring and influencing people. It's "all carrot, no stick." There are also those who lead with "sticks," using coercion to get people to do what they want. Some have the power to coerce—exclusive leadership positions, big-money backing, or even a power player in their pocket. It really doesn't matter if they actually *use* the stick, but when people know it's there, they can be moved to act in ways they otherwise would not.

Coercion is *always a negative force.* It is using pressure to force others to think and act in a certain way by implying or using threats.

By contrast, *influence can be positive.* It's the ability or power to affect others, things, or events without any undue pressure. Internationally recognized leadership expert, speaker, coach, and author John C. Maxwell puts it well, "Leadership is not about titles, positions or flowcharts. It is about one life influencing another."[163] You don't need the charisma of Gandhi, but you do need to know how to effectively communicate with diverse audiences.

In its best form, leadership should influence choices in a positive way. In the Innovation Economy, there is no place for command-and-control direction. Whether on the playing field, in the classroom, or in the community, in the end we all choose our actions. It is the influence of others, not their coercion, that plays a positive role in the choices

---

162 Robert K. Greenleaf, *The Power of Servant-Leadership*, Berrett-Koehler Publishers, Oakland, CA, 1998, 181.
163 John Ramstead, "Characteristics of a Leader," Leadership Coaching, accessed November 30, 2016, http://eternalleadership.com/characteristics-of-a-leader/.

we make. *Inclusive Competitiveness* has to be all about *influencing* disconnected communities, not *coercing* them, to choose to learn about, engage, and successfully compete in the Innovation Economy.

I learned the difference between influence and coercion in community leadership early in my career. It was during a local political issue campaign over a sweeping government reform to fundamentally change the city's form of government to install a "strong mayor." This effort was being led by the big businesses that were trying to *force* citizens to adopt their idea. As such, I labeled it "an unwanted imposition of privileged political will."

The big business-led effort had the hallmarks of community coercion. They avoided all the traditional means of building community support for a new idea, especially one that would have to be adopted by and benefit the voters. Here are some details about these corporate leaders:

- In a richly diverse city, they were all White men.
- They had conceived solely among themselves a local government reform idea that would affect all city residents.
- None of them actually lived in the city.
- They used no community engagement process and received no public input.
- They hired professionals to gather enough signatures to put their issue on the ballot.
- They funded their campaign to the tune of $250,000 with corporate donations, and not a single living *person* (as distinguished from corporation "persons") donated to the campaign.

Clearly, this is not the way to lead a local political initiative.

Relying on influence, the opposition (our side) took a different approach:

- Our campaign was diverse, reflecting the city.
- Our leadership was comprised mostly of city residents.
- We focused on grassroots efforts.
- We raised "enough" money, just about $70,000, with a laser focus on *individual* donors.

The big business leaders thought they had a "stick." We knew we were all "carrot."

Needless to say, we won a landslide electoral victory. The big business proposal was simply bad public policy and their "stick" process even worse than their idea.

Despite their overwhelming advantages, they lost. Our influence beat their coercion.

Upshot: Exert Influence

In this example, we had no stick. We had no ability to *make* anyone do anything. Everything our team did was achieved through influence, which attracted the right collaborators and brought us winning results. *Inclusive Competitiveness* leadership is best when it is about influence, persuasion, and inspiration. Even in cases when it has access to sticks, it should never lead with, use, or even threaten to use them. The single "weapon" of *Inclusive Competitiveness* leadership is its ability to convey a compelling narrative to disconnected communities about challenges and opportunities embedded in the Innovation Economy, influencing them to engage with and successfully compete in it.

PRINCIPLE 7: PROCESS OVER CONTENT

Traditionally, content was the thing on which people, organizations, and institutions primarily focused. It can be described as an individual's narrowly defined specific skills or profession. In an organizational or corporate sense, content means the line or lines of businesses in which the institution or company participates. A content-focused organization states: "We offer education services, period." Or such a corporation might say, "We produce widgets, period."

Of course, disconnected communities need people and organizations that do good things, that have and produce good content. But to make great change happen, such as *Inclusive Competitiveness*, you need another component—a supporting *process* or underlying way to do those things. *Inclusive Competitiveness* embodies new ways of doing old things and, perhaps, more importantly, it involves doing altogether new things in disconnected communities.

Content is the "what" of the equation, where *process* is the "how" or the way to do it.

For *Inclusive Competitiveness* leaders, how they do things can be more important than what they actually do.

The A.O.L. described earlier is a perfect example of process and you can use it for nearly any*thing* you want to accomplish. When you begin to explore *Inclusive Competitiveness* in disconnected communities, you already have the approach: *Aggregate, Organize, Leverage*. Then fit in the particulars of the *IC Framework* and you'll be ready to act. Here's an example that demonstrates the value of process over content.

In Chapter 2, I described my role as new senior staff of a market-leading chamber of commerce, I was given a complex task: to "do something" about regional technology and innovation-based economic development. At the time, I had no real T/IBED experience. All I had was a desk, one half of an administrative assistant and a great organizational platform from which to launch. I brought along a good Rolodex of creative, committed friends, many of whom were already working to help innovative startup companies grow. These friends ranged from local government officials to entrepreneurs to senior executives. This network of friends would prove invaluable to my success.

Applying the A.O.L. process, I asked myself: "Whom do I need to *Aggregate* to help me here? How should I *Organize* them? And how can I *Leverage* all these people and resources to reach my goal?"

I recruited fifteen of the best people I could find. Our task was to make an opportunity assessment for the City of Cincinnati and recommend programs, technologies, and policy innovations that could help make the city a leader in what was then called the "New Economy." The project was named "Fast Break." Our effort was designed to be a start—a catalyst—with my underlying goal to build a lasting regional technology and innovation organization, not just a singular project focused on city government.

The project attracted a good measure of local media interest. Out of the blue, I got a call from a senior executive at Procter & Gamble, a great American company headquartered in Cincinnati. He said: "I just read about your Fast Break project, and I'm wondering why P&G wasn't asked to participate." I responded: "Fast Break is a small, catalytic effort. What we need is a large, regional effort. That's where we really need P&G leadership."

And that began my next round of the A.O.L. process. That P&G senior executive thought our effort had merit, and he encouraged me to keep him apprised of future developments.

At the same time, the chamber of commerce was preparing for its annual business leaders' luncheon. More than 1,000 executives of regionally located (and globally impacting) businesses were all scheduled to be in one room. Fortuitously, the keynote speaker was to be A.G. Lafley, the new CEO of Procter & Gamble!

The P&G team asked the chamber what Lafley should talk about—you can guess what it was! To an audience of many of the area's movers and shakers, Lafley launched a hundred-day effort called the Regional Technology Initiative. This was precisely the lift that my still new role needed.

When I began with the chamber of commerce, a reporter asked me what I was going to do. What he was really asking for was the content of my efforts. I said, "Honestly, I have no idea. But ask me again in six months!" And almost six months to the day, our team was able to describe a new venture, launched by Lafley, P&G, and more than 300 others, resulting in CincyTech—the new voice of technology and innovation in our region.

Upshot: Process is Key

There is no doubt that it was more important to embrace the right process to perform my job over merely focusing on its content. The A.O.L. process led to securing Lafley's and P&G's leadership. This in turn led to the aggregation of more than three hundred volunteers and key resources and assets; the organization of these resources and assets into a hundred-day community initiative; and, finally, these assets and resources were collaboratively leveraged to create a new organization that endures to this day as one of the Midwest's leading startup company accelerators.

For disconnected communities to win this century, their individual and organizational leadership must focus on more than simply content. Instead, they must also develop understanding and appreciation of the underlying processes—through community systems and A.O.L.—that can be deployed into all kinds of Innovation Economy content, specifically: STEM / STEAM education attainment, capital formation and investment, research and commercialization, HGE and entrepreneurship, higher impact employment, and enabling policy.

At the end of the day, *Inclusive Competitiveness* leadership should implement both new content and process in disconnected communities—an overhaul of the "what" and the "how" to improve productivity and quality of life in the Innovation Economy.

PRINCIPLE 8: ENDGAME CONTRIBUTION OVER MIDDLEGAME GRIEVANCE

With the demographically-driven *Inclusive Competitiveness* imperative bearing down on our nation, there are new opportunities to evolve disconnected community leadership from one that is almost exclusively focused on *grievances* to one that includes a necessary and complementary focus on *contribution*.

During grammar school, we all learned that the "subject" of a sentence is something that *does* things, and the "object" is something that has things *done to it*. Since the inception of the U.S., disconnected Americans have struggled to achieve the end goal of becoming subjects of the American economy rather than objects.

Becoming *subjects* of the American economy includes:

- The continued resolution of persistent grievances,
- Acquisition of all rights and privileges that should benefit every American, and
- Acceptance of all responsibilities that come with this position.

As the prolonged lower economic productivity of disconnected Americans demonstrates, the forward thrusts of grievance resolution are only part of the solution. While they are big and necessary steps, they are only the middlegame and not the endgame.

This is a key point: *Inclusive Competitiveness leadership should focus on moving disconnected communities through—and not around—the middlegame to the ultimate endgame to improve economic productivity and quality of life.*

My experience is that many leaders and organizations in disconnected communities work to address legitimate grievances, but far fewer are focused on modern-day economic opportunities. The endgame of *Inclusive Competitiveness* leadership should be all about giving everything to the future potential of disconnected communities. It should help them take full advantage of all rights and privileges and infuse them with the responsibility of making their highest and best *contributions* to the nation's global economic competitiveness. It is the difference between past- and future-focused thinking and activity.

I'm not saying that leaders and organizations that focus mostly on resolving grievances aren't helping to bring about meaningful and much-needed progress. It is clear that they do make a difference. However, this is middlegame progress. *Inclusive Competitiveness* leadership needs to be about the endgame, pursing contribution over grievance.

Its goal is to help disconnected communities take full advantage of all our rights and privileges. It aims to ignite within them the duty to compete hard in the economy. The ultimate purpose is to facilitate better opportunities for disconnected Americans to contribute the best they have to offer, realizing economic benefit for themselves, their families, and communities that is commensurate with those contributions.

Upshot: Keep the Endgame in Focus

There is always a strong pull on leaders and organizations in disconnected communities to redress real injustices. *Inclusive Competitiveness* leadership has to include a measure of "checks and balances" and should never shy away from finding resolution of those grievances. Their redress is indispensable to making one's highest and best contribution. However, with the severe demographic and economic challenges facing our families, communities, and the nation described within these pages, the central focus of *Inclusive Competitiveness* should remain on the endgame: to help disconnected communities to improve their productivity in today's Innovation Economy, thus enhance their quality of life.

PRINCIPLE 9: OPPORTUNITY OVER LEGACY

Legacies are about the past. Opportunities are about the future.

Legacy-based leadership struggles because it is always looking back. At their worst, legacies can keep leaders and organizations from taking advantage of opportunities, and can emphasize past glories at the expense of future possibilities. By distinction, opportunity leadership can honor the past by building a prosperous and productive future.

Consider the American auto industry. It is generally agreed that no American city contributed more to the Allied powers during World War II than Detroit. Appropriately, then, Detroit grew to become known as "The Arsenal of Democracy." However, thirty or so years later, this most profitable industry was on its heels, with global competition eating its lunch.

Bill Gates is famous for saying, "The thing I worry about is some guy in his garage inventing something I haven't thought of." In other words, his potential competitors are those people who are innovating, looking forward—without limits—to what is ahead, to the next great thing.

Opportunity leadership asks the right questions, forms the right strategies, and builds the right organizations to deal with challenges they face today and those they will face tomorrow. Unfortunately, the preponderance of leadership in disconnected communities is legacy-based, dealing with problems rooted in the twentieth century.

In the lobby of a long-standing disconnected community organization in Cleveland, the walls are covered with poster-sized photos of successful moments. This is good. However, each of the pictures is at least twenty years old, and many reflect special moments from the 1960s and 1970s. This organization focused on the proud legacy it had created in the past. And that legacy focus was evident in most of the organization's programs that were things they had done for generations. There is nothing that visibly projects present and future opportunities for the community. There is nothing championing twenty-first century innovation—no evidence of Internet technology, science, engineering, research, and/or laboratories. This is to their detriment.

Sadly, too many leaders in disconnected communities have not learned to focus on the present, let alone the future. Nor have they been afforded the opportunity by government and philanthropic funders (who provide substantial funding for economic competitiveness activities that do not advance inclusion) to do so. And, as detailed earlier, while it's far from perfect, today's Innovation Economy represents the most accessible and merit-based economic period in history. Indeed, we reap what we sow. But few disconnected Americans are sowing the seeds of economic competitiveness.

As I write this, I'm a co-founder of ScaleUp Partners[164]—an opportunity-focused consultancy, not one of legacy. ScaleUp Partners is building a national network of people, community organizations, governments,

---

164 "ScaleUp Partners," accessed November 30, 2016, www.scaleuppartners.com.

K-12 education, universities, and businesses who are tackling the lack of innovation and economic inclusion and competitiveness in disconnected communities across America. Our goal is not to preserve the past, but to authentically honor it by building on the past to secure a promising future.

Upshot: Hunt for Opportunity

Contributions of legacy-focused organizations in disconnected communities are still in great need! Clearly, we have dragged many challenges and problems from the twentieth century into the twenty-first century. Without doubt, there remains a mighty contribution for these leaders and organizations to make today.

Conversely, *Inclusive Competitiveness* leadership builds new community systems designed to create new opportunities for disconnected Americans to contribute to and successfully compete in the twenty-first century economy. These new systems do not replace incumbent legacy efforts. Rather they necessarily complement and enhance them.

PRINCIPLE 10: ALIGNMENT OVER CONSENSUS

The two leading processes for group decision-making are consensus and alignment. Consensus generally involves all members of the group having an equal say in a collaborative activity. The end result of this kind of accord is often an acceptable, rather than breakthrough, resolution. Consensus-building can be a powerfully positive tool to achieve buy-in from diverse parties. However, this process also can contribute to a false sense of group democracy. While all points of view are to be respected in a collaborative process, they do not all have equal value.

Consensus-building processes frequently treat divergent positions as uniformly equal, ensuring a strong possibility that a group's chosen course of action will be the one that is the least objectionable to the largest number of participants. I have observed consensus-building processes regularly resulting in watered down and ineffective actions.

By contrast, alignment is about getting the group to all face and move in the same direction, toward its chosen North Star. It means:

- Making a concerted effort to clarify and help people understand the issues and what their respective responses and roles to address them can be,
- Asking questions and listening to feedback both from the participants, as well as others knowledgeable about or affected by the issues, and
- Making the necessary adjustments in strategy and tactics as conditions change while maintaining fidelity to the North Star.[165]

With alignment processes, everyone has an opportunity to be heard. Then leaders help the group to make clear choices that connect to and strengthen the group's guiding North Star. In this way, the process is more likely to stay on track and choices are more likely to earn real backing from the group.

Over the years, I've spoken to many groups in and serving disconnected communities about *Inclusive Competitiveness*. I greatly enjoy sharing my passion with others on the subject. These meetings tend to follow the same script: I introduce *Inclusive Competitiveness* and begin to lay out approaches to adopt and implement its framework. The topic is well-received. There are great expressions of interest,

---

165 Beatrice Biggs, "Consensus or Alignment?" Institute for Facilitation and Change, accessed November 30, 2016, http://consensusdecisionmaking.org/Articles/Consensus%20or%20Alignment.pdf.

and deep and healthy dialogue ensues. Unfortunately, the discussion begins to devolve from economic inclusion and competitiveness as participants cannot seem to move beyond other real challenges facing disconnected communities, typically including housing, small business services, construction issues, corporate supplier diversity, and government contracting. Then, usually an early consensus begins to emerge that the framework should address all of these and many other issues. Instead of maintaining its focus, *Inclusive Competitiveness* then risks taking on more burden than it can possibly bear and becoming a mishmash of concepts assembled together that lacks clarity and coherence.

It is quite understandable as disconnected communities have had these painful problems for generations and it is what they intimately know. Looking beyond these issues is also often difficult for them because the ideas being presented are new and different and may be perceived as competitive with existing leadership. It is a classic example of sometimes not being able to see the forest for the trees.

This customary scenario highlights key distinctions between achieving consensus and alignment. *Inclusive Competitiveness* leaders have a choice:

- To provide the kind of leadership that aligns with and builds on the *IC Framework* and leading community processes that connect up to and strengthen the framework, or
- To allow the framework to be loaded down with challenges that have merit and reflect the consensus of participants but are not wholly concentrated on economic inclusion and competitiveness.

I always choose alignment over consensus.

Upshot: Choose Alignment

Inclusive Competitiveness should be an integral and complementary part of overall development strategies in disconnected communities, not the single strategy. It was architected to tackle a narrow, but disproportionately impactful set of concerns related to improving productivity in the Innovation Economy. *Inclusive Competitiveness* leadership should acknowledge that the ultimate decision-making standards, against which all matters should be weighed, are The Law of *Inclusive Competitiveness* (discussed in the next chapter) and the *IC Framework*. Together, they are the North Star for economic inclusion and competitiveness. As important as the challenges and opportunities may be, those that do not align with the law and fortify the framework should be addressed through other community leadership.

Consensus can be a useful process of community engagement to address the enormity of the challenges and opportunities facing disconnected Americans and our nation. However, to create productive, vibrant, and inclusive communities in the Innovation Economy, it is essential to move forward by using the principle of alignment to tap into the power for change that is inherent in the leadership principles of *Inclusive Competitiveness* outlined in this chapter.

CHAPTER 8

THE LAW OF INCLUSIVE COMPETITIVENESS

AND BUILDING SUPPORTING COMMUNITY SYSTEMS

There is an economic angst gripping our country. Over the past several years, the need to address the twin troubles of income inequality and staggering wealth disparities has increasingly gained traction in the U.S. We've experienced forty years of continued stagnation of workers' wages. We have witnessed the Occupy Wall Street protest movement and the unforeseen rise of leading presidential contenders Senator Bernie Sanders and Donald Trump—whose campaigns reflected those concerns.

These worries are exacerbated and long-standing among disconnected Americans and in their communities. To adapt a phrase that's popular with community activists, "If America catches cold, then disconnected Americans catch pneumonia!" In other words, whatever economic pain is felt by the nation overall is felt in an exponentially greater way in underserved communities.

To alleviate this fiscal anxiety, transformation is needed in precisely the organizations—governments, philanthropies and nonprofits—that are charged with leading, supporting, and funding efforts to help create new opportunities in disconnected communities. Offering a clear path forward, the Law of *Inclusive Competitiveness* supplies the foundational statement to establish a guiding vision for these communities and the new systems they need to become competitive in the Innovation Economy.

THE LAW OF INCLUSIVE COMPETITIVENESS

Informed by more than thirty years of diverse, high-level leadership experience, The Law of *Inclusive Competitiveness* sets forth the demo-graphically-driven economic inclusion and competitiveness imperative. It provides North Star guidance for those who want to successfully develop and pursue *Inclusive Competitiveness* processes and strategies. Inspired by Packard's Law of Hewlett-Packard Co-Founder, David Packard,[166] The Law of *Inclusive Competitiveness* states:

> No nation can sustainably improve global economic competitiveness without growing exponentially more higher impact employees and higher growth entrepreneurs—which requires the inclusion of disconnected

---

166 Dave Lavinsky, "Which is Worse for Entrepreneurs: Indigestion or Starvation?" growthink, December 29, 2010, accessed December 2, 2016, quoting Packard's Law, "No company can grow revenues consistently faster than its ability to get enough of the right people to implement that growth and still become a great company," http://www.growthink.com/content/which-worse-entrepreneurs-indigestion-or-starvation.

citizens—who create and take advantage of these improved economic conditions.

More like a "law of nature"[167] (rather than any law enforced by courts), the Law of *Inclusive Competitiveness* boils down to a single acknowledgment: that resilient national economic prosperity for the U.S. is only possible when a larger percentage of Americans are higher impact employees who contribute disproportionately more value to their employers (through creative problem-solving and improved productivity) and higher growth entrepreneurs who create jobs at accelerated rates.

Recall that *Inclusive Competitiveness* is an interdisciplinary framework for creating and implementing community systems that improve the economic productivity and quality of life of disconnected Americans. The laser-focus on community systems that are aligned with Innovation Economy priorities distinguishes it from incumbent approaches to community and economic development in disconnected communities.

The Law of *Inclusive Competitiveness* is designed to be the glue, as well as the call to action, to confront the demographically-driven, national economic imperative. This binding of purposes can result in an improvement in economic productivity and the quality of life for disconnected Americans.

The law helps structure community leadership around the *IC Framework* and prevents it from becoming anything other than focused on economic inclusion and competitiveness. It provides guidance for policy, process, and practice actions.

While there is no mechanism to enforce the Law of *Inclusive Competitiveness*, as in civil and criminal law, the articulation of a clear

---

167 "A regularly occurring or apparently inevitable phenomenon observable in human society," Oxford Dictionaries, accessed November 30, 2016, http://www.oxford-dictionaries.com/us/definition/american_english/law-of-nature.

national imperative, combined with the good faith efforts of community leaders to implement the framework, should be sufficient to keep most undertakings on track.

IC FRAMEWORK REVISITED

Before looking at the essentials needed to build supporting community systems it may be helpful to briefly revisit the *IC Framework:*

ENABLING POLICY

Policy is the enabling force of *Inclusive Competitiveness* and creates the requisite conditions for economic inclusion and competitiveness processes, strategies, practices, and metrics.

STRATEGY ELEMENTS

- **Instill New Community Economic Narrative:** Evolve economic culture, leadership, and advocacy in disconnected communities to emphasize economic inclusion and competitiveness.

- **Support New Education Leadership:** Improved STEM / STEAM education attainment will contribute to greater access to innovation and entrepreneurship ecosystems and ultimately to the Innovation Economy.

- **Promote New Organizational Leadership:** New organizational leadership is required to complement (not replace) and build upon incumbent services with new capacities and capabilities that are aligned with local and U.S. economic competitiveness levers and opportunities.

THE IC FRAMEWORK

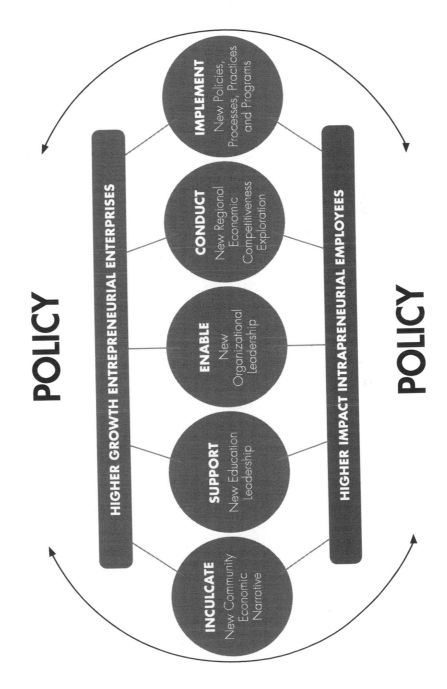

POLICY

POLICY

HIGHER GROWTH ENTREPRENEURIAL ENTERPRISES

HIGHER IMPACT INTRAPRENEURIAL EMPLOYEES

IMPLEMENT New Policies, Processes, Practices and Programs

CONDUCT New Regional Economic Competitiveness Exploration

ENABLE New Organizational Leadership

SUPPORT New Education Leadership

INCULCATE New Community Economic Narrative

- **Conduct New Regional Economic Competitiveness Exploration, Selection and Prioritization:** An appropriate emphasis on *Inclusive Competitiveness* is needed in the early stages of every local economic competitiveness exploration and selection of priority areas of focus.

- **Adopt New Policies, Processes and Practices:** Creative, risk-astute policy, process, and practice advancements across a diverse set of stakeholders are required to activate and sustain *Inclusive Competitiveness*.

DESIRED OUTCOMES

The primary goal of *Inclusive Competitiveness* is to create new economic athletes who fill the dual pipelines of performance and productivity and become the intrapreneurs (employees infused with the principles and ethic of entrepreneurship) and job-creating entrepreneurs our nation needs.

BUILDING SUPPORTING COMMUNITY SYSTEMS

In earlier chapters are detailed accounts that demonstrate the weaknesses of many of the programs prevalent in disconnected communities. These narrowly tailored, direct-service programs are generally disconnected from regional, state, and national economic competitiveness priorities. Place-based approaches[168] that focus on preferences for awarding federal government contracts and tax incentives for hiring

---

168 Examples: Small Business Administration's Historically Underutilized Business Zones (HUBZone) program, https://www.sba.gov/contracting/government-contracting-programs/hubzone-program/understanding-hubzone-program, and Housing and Urban Development's Empowerment Zones program, https://www.hudexchange.info/programs/ez/.

residents of distressed communities are helpful. However, they also fall short of improving the economic productivity and quality of life for a large percentage of disconnected Americans.

Sustainable community systems (or ecosystems) concentrated on employment and entrepreneurship in the Innovation Economy is essential to the solution. Effectively applying the *IC Framework* in disconnected communities will help remedy this problem.

GOOD IDEAS ARE EVERYWHERE

In Chapter 7, I recounted that in 2001 I had the honor to work with A.G. Lafley, former chairman, president, and CEO of P&G. He helped launch a project I led named the Regional Technology Initiative, which resulted in CincyTech, a leading innovation company accelerator. He was also chairman of the relevant leadership council comprised of the area's university presidents, elected officials, and leading CEOs. Dubbed the Angel Board, it took on responsibilities akin to an angel investor, providing guidance and financial and other backing to our startup effort.

During one of our talks, Lafley shared that more than 90 percent of P&G innovation originated in-house. I was silently and suitably impressed. Then he totally stunned me with this statement: "We have to get that percentage down." I'm not sure if it showed on my face, but I was baffled.

Lafley explained that almost all of P&G's innovation was from within the company and that he wanted to begin to lower the amount of internal innovation and increase the external innovation by tapping into the company's global network of partners and suppliers. His explanation immediately resonated with me. Familiar with Napoleon Hill's Mastermind theory of organizing disparate, interdisciplinary knowledge among multiple people and uniting it to attain a common and definite purpose,[169] Lafley's description sounded to me like P&G was going to build one big global brain to improve the company's innovation.

When Lafley took the helm at P&G in 2000, the company had ten billion-dollar brands. By the time he retired in 2009, the company had increased that figure to an impressive twenty-three billion-dollar brands.[170] He is viewed as the most successful CEO in P&G history[171] and his accomplishments eventuated through a focus on innovation.

Similarly, the *IC Framework* is not concerned about where broadly-defined innovation comes from. Its goal is to open new opportunities for both the connected and disconnected to contribute to improving the economic productivity and quality of life of Americans who have not yet been a part of the Innovation Economy. Indeed, the framework can help build one big, interdisciplinary brain to improve community innovation and economic competitiveness.

DEVELOPING A PROCESS ORIENTATION

From neighborhoods to communities to regional environments, when it comes to economic development and improving competitiveness almost everyone instantly wants outstanding outcomes or products. And rightly so. After all, there are often strong needs, a long history of doing things a particular way (and without obtaining the desired results) or leaders simply may be unaware of other ways to achieve goals. I call this phenomenon "The Tyranny of Outcomes."

---

169 Napoleon Hill, *Think and Grow Rich*, Wilder Publications, Radford, VA, September 10, 2007,: https://www.amazon.co.uk/Think-Grow-Rich-Napoleon-Hill/dp/193 4451355/277-5764436-8705950?ie=UTF8&keywords=think%20and%20grow% 20rich&qid=1424854954&ref_=sr_1_1&s=books&sr=1-1.

170 Rance Crain, "A.G. Lafley's Shares His Secret for P&G Success: Slow Down, Focus on Fundamentals," Advertising Age, August 6, 2012, accessed December 2, 2016, http://adage.com/article/rance-crain/a-g-lafley-s-shares-secret-p-g-success/236472/.

171 Ghazal Hashemipour, "A.G. Lafley: A Look Back at the Career of the Most Successful CEO in P&G History" Chief Executive, June 13, 2016, accessed December 2, 2016, http://chiefexecutive.net/g-lafley-look-back-career-successful-ceo-pg-history/.

When these outcomes are the singular focus, there is a problem. What is needed is the specific creation of higher impact, intrapreneurial employees and higher growth, job-creating entrepreneurs. However, it is quite difficult to reach these *Inclusive Competitiveness* outcomes without consideration of either community processes or resources that are required for sustainable efforts and longer-term impact.

Time and time again, throughout my career, I have heard influential policymaking leaders make statements such as: "We are not interested in process and activities. We are about outcomes!" Unfortunately, this shortsighted approach obstructs the realization of their important and well-intended goals. Without following the crucial steps of first undertaking community process—which leads to the creation of new community policy—what invariably follows is this: specialists, like me, who are called upon to facilitate the changes, experience the very real struggle to find the necessary resources (including human and financial) to achieve those outcomes.

It is the same as asking for outputs without the requisite inputs or attending to the effect of a matter without ever addressing the cause.

Recognizing the necessity of community process, *Inclusive Competitiveness* embodies the credo "no product before process."

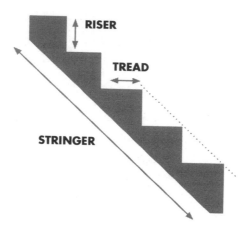

As illustrated, reaching desired *Inclusive Competitiveness* results or products is like climbing a stairway– specific activities (tread) lead to a set of outcomes (riser), which creates new opportunities for new activities (tread) that lead to a new set of outcomes (riser) ... and so on. Activities and outcomes build one on top of the other and are all connected together and aligned (stringer) pointing toward the North Star of *economic inclusion and competitiveness.*

In law school, we were taught that a "condition precedent" is an event or state of affairs that is required *before* something else will occur. Community process is the condition precedent that is needed to improve community outcomes. Achieving *Inclusive Competitiveness* results require on-going development and implementation, repeatedly, of specific actions and behaviors.

Importantly, *Inclusive Competitiveness* processes need the same kind and level of human and financial investment for their activities as are provided for the market-leading economic development and competitiveness organizations that steward local innovation and entrepreneurship ecosystems. Without these commensurate investments, community processes will not sustain and be able to advance *Inclusive Competitiveness.*

IDENTIFYING PROBLEMS AND WORKING ON SOLUTIONS

In medicine, the process of identifying a medical condition or disease by its signs, symptoms, and from the results of various analytic procedures is called diagnosing. Typically, a person with abnormal symptoms will consult a physician, who will then obtain a history of the patient's illness and examine him/her for signs of disease. The physician will formulate a hypothesis of a likely diagnosis and provide treatment for the ailment. The doctor generally has a prescriptive framework to inform her assessment.

Diagnosis is needed to determine problems and verify their causes.

Similarly, the *IC Framework* provides the foundation on which a proper diagnosis can be made and an effective treatment plan (strategy) developed to create new community systems to connect the disconnected to the Innovation Economy.

Complementing the diagnosis is the discovery process. The field of law discovery is wide-ranging and can involve any information or material which is relevant to the case, except that which is privileged. Importantly, most civil cases are settled after discovery. At that time, both sides are often in agreement about the relative strengths and weaknesses of the case. This regularly results in an equitable settlement and eliminates the expense and risks of a trial. Both sides discover together and together they recognize solutions.

Discovery is all about uncovering solutions to address the causes and problems that have been diagnosed.

The *IC Framework* informs the community discovery process. During discovery, disconnected communities join with connected local, state, and national economic development and competitiveness leaders, as well as human, education, and business services providers. Together, they are able to jointly explore the challenges and opportunities to improve productivity in the Innovation Economy.

Similar to the practice of law, after discovery, both those connected to the Innovation Economy and those disconnected can come together to jointly uncover, recognize, and implement solutions.

The introspective processes of prescriptive diagnosis and joint discovery are the condition precedent. Their undertaking will greatly enhance prospects for finding agreement and alignment about the relative challenges and opportunities of implementing the *IC Framework*.

COMING TOGETHER AND BUILDING ECOSYSTEMS

Generally, the Eight Communities of Influence (8 COI)[172] should comprise local economic inclusion and competitiveness ecosystems. The following diagram provides a useful perspective for identifying interdisciplinary assets and is meant to serve as a general guide. The 8 COI all play (or can play) a role in, and have (or can have) an impact upon, the economic competitiveness of any given area, region, or community.

---

172 Created by Mike Green, Co-founder, ScaleUp Partners, 2013, www.scaleuppartners. com.

EIGHT COMMUNITIES OF INFLUENCE (8 COI)

Created by Mike Green, Cofounder, ScaleUp Partners, 2013

EDUCATION	COMMUNITY	POLICY	FUNDING
K-12 Public Schools Charter/Private Schools Faith-Based Schools Vocational Schools Community Colleges Universities	Social/Health Orgs Community Development Housing/Residential Faith-Based Non-Government Orgs Parent/Student Groups Fraternities/Sororities Legacy Nonprofits	Government Public-Private Alliances Foundations Professional Associations Elected/Appointed Officials Wealthy/Powerful Individuals	Government/Taxpayers Banks/Financial Orgs Foundations Pensions Private Equity Venture Capital Angel Investors Crowdfunders

DEVELOPMENT	INDUSTRY	ENTREPRENEURS	COMMUNICATIONS
Economic Development Tech-Based Econ Dev Regional Dev Orgs/CEDS Planning Real Estate Development Public-Private Partners Faith-Based Econ Dev Universities	Corporations Mature Large/Small Biz Succesful Startups Gazelles Professional Associations Fraternities/Sororities	Entrepreneurs Associations Incubators Accelerators Conference/Competitions Activities/Meetups Hackathons Startup Weekends	Media Public Relations Corporations Government Foundations Policymakers Newsmakers/Pundits Columnists

Once convened, this group will engage in the diagnosis and discovery processes to analyze and explore the local economic competitiveness landscape. These include existing strategies and plans in their area and around the country designed to improve:

- Education outcomes,
- Tech-based workforce opportunities,
- Entrepreneurship,
- Job growth,
- Wealth creation, and
- Overall well-being of community members.

Further, the 8 COI establish the most promising practices for identifying, developing, and implementing key strategies for implementing the *IC Framework*.

IDENTIFYING AND BUILDING OPPORTUNITIES WITH SYSTEM MAPPING

System mapping,[173] as a process, helps communities cope with complexity and aligns investment with high-leverage interventions that have the best opportunities for impact. The system map is an interconnected set of activity-nodes used to illustrate and clarify the behavior within the local economic competitiveness system: each node represents a different action which can be taken to achieve one or more economic competitiveness objectives. The dynamism and interconnectivity of the system map distinguishes it from the traditional and static asset

---

173 Based on the model developed by Bush Consulting Group, NorTech and ScaleUp Partners (formerly The America21 Project).

map. The latter usually only provides an inventory of the strengths and resources of a community and is generally depicted in linear form.[174]

The system map a) helps highlight the intersection points of complex (and often non-obvious) relationships and b) provides a baseline for informing individual decisions, or actions, with regard to the entire economic competitiveness system. The 8 COI's prescriptive diagnosis and joint discovery processes begin with system mapping.

Critical to the process is constructing a system map with connected and disconnected community stakeholders, which will provide a common framework to facilitate shared understanding and stimulate diagnosis and discovery. This concurrently exposes both connected and disconnected communities to the challenges and opportunities inherent in the local economic competitiveness vision and strategy.

Connected and disconnected community participants are essential to the success of the system mapping process. Each is needed to:

- Contribute high-quality content during the process (in the form of system mapping inputs) and
- Serve as a steering body and be the eventual recipients of, and decisive advocates for, the resulting intervention strategies.

The system mapping process also ensures tight alignment to these strategies. A clear line of sight can be drawn to indicate activities that can support local economic competitiveness priorities and indicate which activities should or shouldn't be pursued. As a result, the process encourages broad ownership of a narrowly defined set of concrete deliverables, milestones, and rationale for action against the system map's well-defined starting point.

---

174 UCLA Center for Health Policy Research, Health DATA Program – Data, Advocacy and Technical Assistance, http://healthpolicy.ucla.edu/programs/health-data/trainings/Documents/tw_cba20.pdf.

THE SYSTEM MAP DELIVERS:

- An action plan with clear rationale for selecting specific areas of focus, action, and investment of scarce resources,

- Descriptions of specific existing and new high-impact interventions that will help connected and disconnected community organizations better advance economic inclusion and competitiveness,

- Identification of high-impact interventions already taking place locally that have potential for scaled outcomes,

- Assignment of individual organizations or a collective group of organizations to be accountable for implementing high-impact economic inclusion and competitiveness interventions,

- Outcome and performance metrics to measure individual and collective organizational performance and impact, and

- An estimate of costs associated with implementing high-impact economic inclusion and competitiveness interventions.

The System Map Delivers More Than Traditional Approaches as It:

- Enables several organizations to achieve both greater individual and collective impact,

- Identifies, aligns, and enhances proven activities that can "move the needle,"

- Creates new programs and strategic initiatives that will help improve the productivity of disconnected communities through education attainment, business development, job creation, and employment growth,

- Determines specific, high-impact interventions with the greatest positive effect on economic inclusion and competitiveness,

- Improves social, education, and economic outcomes through connected and disconnected partners who can create new efficiencies within an often inefficient, fragmented local economy,

- Strengthens the capacity of each partner organization to leverage local funding to attract additional and out-of-town investment for the most promising efforts, and

- Advances policies, strategies, practices, and metrics across a diverse set of incumbent and new stakeholders that will support demonstration projects, experimentation, and broad dissemination of findings and outcomes.

EMBEDDING INCLUSIVE COMPETITIVENESS

For optimum and sustained impact, *Inclusive Competitiveness* must be embedded into the existing local economic competitiveness strategies and priorities and not be relegated to an ancillary or collateral goal. This is an important key to advancing *IC Framework* objectives because these existing strategies and priorities, in most cases, have been thoroughly vetted by the area's economic competitiveness leaders and generally represent the top opportunities.

The system mapping process described above provides all those involved with a method for deconstructing and simplifying the complex set of interrelated objectives, activities, and relationships that exist within the local economy. It is an immersion process that can significantly increase prospects for sustained economic inclusion and competitiveness action by:

- Deeply educating disconnected communities and organizations about economic competitiveness and aligning their programs and strategies with the local economic competitiveness priorities,

- Determining what connected and disconnected communities value and how their leadership organizations can best individually and collectively advance economic inclusion and competitiveness, and

- Intentionally connecting historically disconnected assets and resources to the region's leading economic competitiveness priorities.

BECOMING INCLUSIVE ...

The delicate and complex nature of system mapping for local economic inclusion and competitiveness cannot be underestimated. Tremendous value is derived from engaging a variety of stakeholders who normally operate in silos, with their work isolated from on-the-ground community problems or disconnected from regional economic competitiveness leadership, organizations, and objectives. These participants no doubt will have widely varying viewpoints on the best courses of action or priorities for meeting local economic competitiveness and/or inclusion aims. The various conversations will likely yield divergent outcomes that will have to be carefully integrated into a single map to ultimately yield one set of priorities with majority buy-in and ownership. Herein lies the strength of this comprehensive system mapping approach.

I have experienced and observed fits and starts related to economic inclusion all over the U.S. I can tell you that this subject seems to carry the unique burden of perceived and real local fatigue, wherein communities may feel they've been addressing this problem for generations without much success. The perception that this may be an intractable problem that cannot be overcome demands the utmost care in the construction, ordering, and facilitation of system mapping. It needs to be treated as a sober and serious community process. An important objective of the system mapping process is to ensure productive, collaborative dialogue and concurrent learning about economic competitiveness challenges and opportunities among all participants. This objective should pervade the process, from inception through subsequent and nuanced revisions and ultimately to conclusion of the system map.

Keep in mind that because a system map can encompass such a large universe of possible activities and players, care must be used to define the system objectives up-front, as well as the various strategies and players whose involvement could feasibly affect the outcome.

BUILDING ON EARLY PROMISE

There are many early ventures to grow the number of locally owned enterprises led by disconnected Americans. These efforts include:

- The provision of seed investments in tech-based companies run by minority or female entrepreneurs,
- Establishment of more business incubators and accelerators in inner cities and rural areas,
- An increase in social capital for disconnected entrepreneurs,
- Generally scaling rural, minority, and women-owned businesses, and
- Waging of campaigns to introduce new and diverse images of successful entrepreneurs.

These tactics address real challenges. However, in three ways they fail to adhere to the process before product (and progress) orientation, rendering them insufficient to meet the needs of disconnected communities in today's economy.

First, while welcomed and needed, few, if any, of these efforts have invested in diagnosis and discovery processes and system mapping with the 8 COI in both connected and disconnected communities. Good resources are being provided to help disconnected entrepreneurs, but there are few or no plans to build broader community capacity, providing them with the awareness, tools, and opportunities needed to continuously conceive, develop, expand, and sustain their businesses for the Innovation Economy. The community narrative is missing. For example, 96 percent of Black-owned and 91 percent of Hispanic businesses do not have employees.[175] Moreover, respectively, these businesses average about $20,000 and $30,000 revenue (sales/receipts).[176] The problem with entrepreneurship in disconnected communities includes, but does not begin or end with, access to capital. Fundamentally, the problem is utter absence in these communities of the kind of economic competitiveness narratives and systems–the *IC Framework*–that over time can reliably produce the job-creating entrepreneurs and enterprises that these communities and the nation sorely need.

Second, natural world ecosystems are generally *organically* created. Innovation and entrepreneurship ecosystems are always *intentionally* created. These systems are the resultant products from deliberate processes. There are no exceptions. As much as they are needed, the current thrust of investments dedicated to supporting disconnected entrepreneurs does not address the absence of economic inclusion and competitiveness systems in disconnected communities. Accordingly, without intentional leadership, economic inclusion and competitiveness systems will not just miraculously appear. This begs the question, how will "inclusive innovation and entrepreneurship" resiliently thrive without new economic inclusion and competitiveness systems to fuel them?

---

175 "2012 Survey of Business Owners," U.S. Census, December 15, 2015, accessed November 30, 2016,
http://factfinder.census.gov/faces/tableservices/jsf/pages/productview.xhtml?pid=S-BO_2012_00CSA01&prodType=table.
176 Ibid.

Finally, perhaps the most perilous of the three weaknesses of current approaches is that when they do not deliver the results hoped for, the risk is extraordinarily high that stakeholders could conclude that "disconnected communities simply don't get innovation. They can't be economically competitive. We tried, but *they* just don't get it." And like Pontius Pilate of two thousand years ago, they may take water, wash their hands, and simply walk away from supporting and investing in the economic inclusion and competitiveness of disconnected Americans. This tragic situation is the outcome of a lack of leadership and vision at the early stage to do the hard, unglamorous work to build community capacity to resiliently compete economically.

Of course, in the areas of both economic competitiveness and *Inclusive Competitiveness*, there are no guarantees. No locked-down assurances that desired outcomes will be achieved. And by the very nature of innovation, you hit some, hopefully a few big ones, and you miss many others.

What is abundantly clear, however, is that disconnected Americans will not improve productivity and enhance their quality of life in today's Innovation Economy without new community systems of economic inclusion and competitiveness. The old ways are becoming quickly outdated and in most cases simply do not work or provide the needed change.

In the words of the U.S. EDA: "First and foremost is the realization that an innovation and entrepreneurship ecosystem is what generates local companies and industries in a systemic and consistent manner ... and that this ecosystem will sustain, so this will continue year after year after year, and startups will continue to grow."[177]

---

177 Nish Acharya, i6 Grant Challenge Informational Session, U.S. Economic Development Administration, Raw Transcript, June 19, 2012, https://www.eda.gov/oie/ris/i6/2012/20120619_informational_session.htm.

10 AREAS AND QUESTIONS
COMMUNITIES SHOULD EXPLORE

While it would be wonderful to say that there are magic or instant answers to challenges faced by disconnected Americans, the reality of course is that there are not. Nevertheless, with the right focus and determination, communities can come together and move toward economic competitiveness and inclusion. Below are ten questions that are extremely helpful for starting the diagnosis and discovery processes the right way:

1. Are there specific foundational competencies related to education, training, and career and professional development that are needed for disconnected populations and communities to be successful across local economic competitiveness industries and occupations?

2. How does the Innovation Economy Squeeze (the top-down pressure of global competition for jobs and the bottom-up pressure of technology adoption [automation], with fewer workers producing more products and services) further distress disconnected populations and communities? What are promising ways to build the complementary dual pipelines of productivity—higher impact employees and higher growth entrepreneurs—that create new economic athletes who can win in this environment?

3. Is there information available that depicts the ways in which disconnected populations and communities are impacted by, and can positively interact with, larger local economic competitiveness programs, initiatives, and structures?

4. What are the key elements of robust, interdisciplinary economic inclusion and competitiveness ecosystems that can support

improved productivity of disconnected populations and communities?

5. What are the most promising ways to reach disconnected populations and communities with new economic narratives? What will be the narratives? How do we communicate them?

6. How should public and private sector policymakers be engaged to better support *Inclusive Competitiveness*?

7. How are the deep, diverse, and unique experiences of both connected and disconnected communities taken into account to properly frame the overall *Inclusive Competitiveness* work?

8. What current research, literature, and existing models demonstrate the link between improving economic productivity of disconnected populations and communities and increased local, regional, and national economic competitiveness?

9. What are the barriers and incentives associated with connecting disconnected populations and communities to the local economic competitiveness priority areas? How can they be empowered to overcome these barriers and take advantage of these incentives to successfully compete?

10. What are the most promising, replicable, and scalable ways—policies, processes, practices, and programs—for local innovation and entrepreneurship ecosystems to help disconnected populations and communities connect to and successfully compete in the local economic competitiveness priority areas?

These foundational areas and opening questions provide an overall context for the community's prescriptive diagnosis and joint discovery process and definitively align the effort with the North Star of economic inclusion and competitiveness.

IGNITING NEW BEHAVIORS

New community behaviors are most often needed to create, sustain, and ultimately achieve the desired outcomes of *Inclusive Competitiveness*. The intended outcome of the exploration process with the 8 COI is to catalyze or otherwise activate these new behaviors.

The process is intended to include the conversations, planning, action, and investment supporting local economic competitiveness priority areas and strategies *and,* of equal importance, focus on the issues of economic inclusion and competitiveness. Essentially, the diagnosis and discovery process with the 8 COI represents not only a pathway to prosperity for those who often have been bypassed by traditional and leading local economic development and competitiveness strategies, but is also a key to preserving and enhancing local economic competitiveness.

CHAPTER 9

FEDERAL LEADERSHIP FOR A NEW NATIONAL INITIATIVE

There is no easy way to tackle the economic disconnection and lack of competitiveness that affect so many parts of our country. Increasingly, the nation is waking up to the gravity of threat posed by, and the urgent need for massive action on, staggeringly lower economic productivity for so many Americans. Solutions require structural change on a national scale and real investment targeted to tapping the latent potential of these Americans.

Current inertia and indifference of our leaders is putting the nation's sustained prosperity at risk. Continued inaction comes at a high cost. Eventually, this failure to act will not only be felt by those who can provide leadership in this area now, it will inevitably undermine the global economic competitiveness of the U.S.

The approach of using siloed, disparate programs has been the dominant paradigm of employment and business development in disconnected communities. Unfortunately, most of these programs are not aligned with the top opportunities our nation has to offer.

The time has come for a national response to tackle this national problem head-on. A countrywide initiative to respond to the challenges and opportunities of economic inclusion and competitiveness could ensure that collaborators across the nation fundamentally understand what it takes to successfully compete in the Innovation Economy. In this new paradigm collaborators learn how to assume new roles and responsibilities and build new relationships and structures. The result: enduring community systems that can improve the productivity and quality of life for disconnected Americans.

There is a single entity in the U.S. with the depth of resources and breadth of experience across multiple sectors of our economy that can *catalyze Inclusive Competitiveness* throughout our nation–that entity is the federal government.

FEDERAL LEADERSHIP

When it comes to innovation and economic competitiveness, the U.S. government plays a huge role. In fact, President Obama's 2017 budget provides $152 billion for American innovation, including research and development and STEM education.[178]

Historically, these investments have returned meaningful dividends. For example, Rosabeth Moss Kanter, professor of business at Harvard Business School, reminds us that "What many people forget is that freewheeling Silicon Valley filled with entrepreneurs was made possible

---

178 "President's 2017 Budget Invests in American Innovation: R&D, Innovation, and STEM Education," Office of Science and Technology Policy Fact Sheet, February 9, 2016, accessed November 30, 2016, https://www.whitehouse.gov/sites/default/files/microsites/ostp/ostp_fact_sheet_2017_budget_final.pdf.

by large defense funding for research and development that led to the semiconductor that led to nearly everything else."[179]

Former U.S. Secretary of Commerce Penny Pritzker, in describing the federal government's role, says that "in order to strengthen our position as the most competitive country in the world, we must seek out new opportunities for American ingenuity to thrive in the global marketplace, creating greater prosperity for the American people." She goes on to say that "one way to ensure American businesses and workers remain competitive is by increasing our investment in [twenty-first century] skills training programs and business development programs for American workers and businesses."

Bruce Katz of the Brookings Institution sums it up this way: the federal government's role in innovation should help accelerate and broaden the impact of innovative growth through community revitalization, and social opportunity.[180] Katz encourages the federal government to do for cities, metros, and disconnected communities what they cannot do for themselves—provide a strong national platform for financial investment in local networks and ecosystems.[181] Disconnected communities cannot create this infrastructure without this national support.

Clearly, the federal government has been and should continue to be an indispensable partner in investing in the innovation and economic competitiveness of the nation. These investments have

---

179 "The Experts: What Role Does Government Play in Spurring Innovation?" The Journal Reports: Leadership, *The Wall Street Journal*, April 21, 2013, accessed November 30, 2016, http://www.wsj.com/articles/SB1000142412788732339330457836023122812 8580.

180 Bruce Katz, "What Should the Role of the Federal Government Be in Supporting Innovation Districts?" *Brookings Institution Paper*, October 8, 2014, accessed November 30, 2016, http://www.brookings.edu/research/papers/2014/10/08-federal-government-in-novation-districts-katz.

181 Ibid.

generated meaningful returns to the economy and are part of fulfilling the government's constitutional duty to promote the general welfare of all Americans.

THE ESSENTIAL CATALYST

An effective federal government policy regime and investment are essential to solve the challenges we have to our economic inclusion and competitiveness. What's needed is a new federal government declaration that *Inclusive Competitiveness* is an important public objective, which is consistent with the legacy of federal, conditions-creating leadership in economic competitiveness. Such a national policy would ignite the kinds of new, private sector activities that are needed to successfully implement the *IC Framework*: the provision of real investment and large-scale intervention to catalyze and sustain new, on-the-ground activity in disconnected communities throughout the U.S.

CENTERS OF EXCELLENCE

A particularly powerful way we've seen federal government investment fortify the U.S. global economic position and spur innovation is through the creation of Centers of Excellence (COEs). A COE can be defined as a "premier organization providing an exceptional product or service in an assigned sphere of expertise and within a specific field of technology, business, or government, aligned with the unique requirements and capabilities of the COE parent organization."[182] Here are several examples:

---

182 William Craig, Matthew Fisher, Suzanne Garcia-Miller, Clay Kaylor, John Porter, and L. Scott Reed, "Generalized Criteria and Evaluation Method for Center of Excellence: A Preliminary Report," Carnegie Mellon University and Software Engineering Institute, December 2009, accessed November 30, 2016, http://repository.cmu.edu/cgi/viewcontent.cgi?article=1287&context=sei.

DEPARTMENT OF COMMERCE

As a non-regulatory federal agency within the U.S. Department of Commerce,[183] the mission of the National Institute of Standards and Technology (NIST) is "to promote U.S. innovation and industrial competitiveness by advancing measurement science, standards, and technology in ways that enhance economic security and improve our quality of life."[184] The NIST COEs expand the agency's impact and delivery of its mission by:

- Enabling it to partner with the private sector, including leading research institutes across the country in emerging technology,
- Enhancing technical innovation,
- Providing new opportunities for training students, and
- Engaging with entrepreneurs and industry.[185]

DEPARTMENT OF HOMELAND SECURITY

The Department of Homeland Security (DHS) COEs network is an extended consortium of hundreds of universities conducting groundbreaking research to address homeland security challenges. It works closely with academia, industry, DHS operational components, and first responders to develop customer-driven, innovative tools and technologies to solve real-world challenges.[186] Importantly, the DHS COEs are also committed to workforce development by educating

---

183 "General Information," *The National Institute of Standards and Technology*, accessed November 30, 2016, http://www.nist.gov/public_affairs/general_information.cfm.

184 "Mission," *The National Institute of Standards and Technology*, accessed November 30, 2016, http://www.nist.gov/public_affairs/mission.cfm.

185 *The National Institute of Standards and Technology Center of Excellence*, accessed November 30, 2016, http://www.nist.gov/coe/.

186 *The Department of Homeland Security Centers of Excellence Network*, accessed November 30, 2016, https://showcase.hsuniversityprograms.org/about/about/.

and training students and professionals in science and engineering disciplines.[187]

NATIONAL ADDITIVE MANUFACTURING INNOVATION INSTITUTE

Growing jobs that pay good wages is undoubtedly the best way to construct our economy to globally compete in the twenty-first century and sustain America's role as a world magnet of opportunity. To this end, the federal government has taken a prominent role in investing in American innovation to strengthen the manufacturing base and keep our nation at the forefront of technological advancement.[188]

Following the proven path of establishing mission-critical COEs, in 2012 the Obama Administration launched a new public-private institute for manufacturing innovation called the National Additive Manufacturing Innovation Institute (NAMII).[189] The NAMII is the pilot institute of President Obama's plan to invest $1 billion to create a National Network of Manufacturing Innovation of up to fifteen COEs around the country. With the goal to become a global COE, the NAMII provides the innovation infrastructure needed to support new additive manufacturing[190] technology and products. These COEs would serve

---

187 Ibid.
188 "Middle Class Economics: Investing in American Innovation, The President's Budget, Fiscal Year 2016," accessed November 30, 2016, https://www.whitehouse.gov/sites/default/files/omb/budget/fy2016/assets/fact_sheets/investing-in-american-in-novation.pdf.
189 "We Can't Wait: Obama Administration Announces New Public-Private Partnership to Support, The White House," Office of the Press Secretary, August 16, 2012, accessed November 30, 2016, https://www.whitehouse.gov/the-press-office/2012/08/16/we-can-t-wait-obama-administration-announces-new-public-private-partners.
190 Additive manufacturing refers to a process by which digital 3D design data is used to build up a component in layers by depositing material. The term "3D printing" is increasingly used as a synonym for Additive manufacturing. http://www.eos.info/additive_manufacturing/for_technology_interested.

as regional hubs of manufacturing excellence that will help to make our manufacturers more competitive and encourage investment in the U.S.[191]

Anchored by a diverse collection of forty companies, nine research universities, five community colleges, and eleven nonprofit organizations,[192] the interdisciplinary NAMII has shown great promise. In just its first year, the NAMII established itself as a nationally-recognized COE for additive manufacturing.[193]

These and other multi-partner, collaborative COEs provide the federal government, and the nation, needed public-private partnership platforms for accelerating innovation and economic competitiveness in myriad fields that achieve enduring global advantages. Moreover, the proven COE model is instructive for launching a national initiative to advance economic inclusion and competitiveness.

PUSH-DOWN AND PULL-DOWN ECONOMICS VS. TRICKLE-DOWN ECONOMICS

Despite the federal government's significant investment of all American taxpayers' dollars into innovation and economic competitiveness, not all Americans have enjoyed the job and enterprise creation benefits of those investments. The nation's investments to date have not broadly translated into new community systems to increase economic prosperity in all parts of the U.S. It seems that when it comes to innovation and economic competitiveness, we are following the trickle-down approach.

---

191 "We Can't Wait: Obama Administration Announces New Public-Private Partnership to Support," accessed November 30, 2016, https://www.whitehouse.gov/the-press-office/2012/08/16/we-can-t-wait-obama-administration-announces-new-public-private-partners.

192 Ibid.

193 "NAMII Commemorates First Anniversary," accessed November 30, 2016, https://www.americamakes.us/news-events/press-releases/item/318-namii-commemorates-first-anniversary.

The premise that national economic growth and prosperity will *naturally* flow to benefit all Americans, including the most disadvantaged and disconnected populations, does not apply here. If I've learned anything in my career—and what I know for sure—is that without *intentionality* to ensure the flow of economic prosperity inures to the benefit of all Americans, the best opportunities will not *naturally* reach disconnected Americans throughout the nation.

This is tantamount to the federal government encouraging disconnected Americans to sit back and wait for others to *get around* to innovating and creating the job and business opportunities that we all need to prosper! This kind of *help* conflicts with the very core of what it means to be American. Our nation's founders didn't *wait* for England to get around to conceding their unalienable rights; Blacks didn't *wait* for Whites to get around to recognizing their human and civil rights; women didn't *wait* for men to get around to admitting their equality; and lesbian, gay, bisexual, and transgender Americans didn't *wait* for straight Americans to get around to extending to them all rights of American citizenship.

Americans don't wait for opportunity. It's just not part of our national character. Rather, we reach up, grab it, and do incredible things with it.

So, why should disconnected Americans be expected to wait for others to act to secure their improved economic future and quality of life? The simple answer is that they should not.

It's important to note that these economically marginalized groups are generally disregarded in matters related to U.S. global economic competitiveness.

There is a vicious cycle here: these disconnected Americans are disregarded in matters of economic competitiveness because they have been educationally and economically less competitive. Meanwhile, there is conspicuous absence of the essential community systems that support the opportunity-to-innovation connection for them to become more competitive. This cycle can and must be disrupted.

The *IC Framework* provides the needed alternative to the customary practices of our nation's current trickle-down innovation and economic competitiveness policies and practices. The framework intentionally complements and enhances existing advocacy, leadership, investment, and services in disconnected communities. It delivers new functions, strategies, and mechanisms to empower and equip these Americans to resolutely reach up and "pull down" the nation's best Innovation Economy opportunities for themselves. Moreover, the framework provides an effective tool for the stewards atop local and regional innovation and entrepreneurship ecosystems to purposefully "push down" the best economic opportunities toward disconnected Americans—through proactive policies and practices—making them more visible, accessible and attainable.

A vital dynamic system is set up when enlightened leadership from our nation's Innovation Economy superstructure "pushes down" so that more disconnected Americans are able to become more competitive and "pull down" new opportunities from the national economy. This will result in increased economic productivity and improved quality of life across the nation.

In the end, disconnected Americans will not prosper without more growth and development of the nation's Innovation Economy. Conversely, the nation's Innovation Economy is only tenuously sustained without the inclusion of disconnected Americans. Accordingly, moving from "trickle-down" to "push-down" and "pull-down" economic policies, strategies, and practices can materially advance economic inclusion and competitiveness in the U.S.

A NEW NATIONAL STRATEGIC INITIATIVE

Sir Isaac Newton's First Law of Motion states that an object at rest stays at rest.[194] As this book details, when it comes to creating new community systems to improve the productivity and quality of life of disconnected Americans in the Innovation Economy, the nation mostly has been at rest.

Newton's Second Law states that a force is needed to catalyze and accelerate a resting mass into motion.[195] A federal strategic initiative represents the kind of force that can ignite and power the national mass into action on economic inclusion and competitiveness, overcoming inertia and resistance to change.[196] To this end, a new national strategic initiative needs to be designed and launched to activate efforts in the U.S. to improve global economic competitiveness through increased productivity of disconnected Americans.

I propose that the development of *The National Inclusive Competitiveness Centers of Excellence* (NICCOE) be that catalytic, strategic initiative - a U.S. "moonshot."

The NICCOE, in essence, acts as an economic rocket booster. Just as boosters on the space shuttle carry the weight of the entire craft pre-launch and provide the immense power to lift the vehicle into space, the NICCOE would be the force to launch, elevate, and fuel a new U.S. economic inclusion and competitiveness strategy. It would establish a new norm, pushing revitalization efforts in disconnected

---

194 Robert S. Kaplan and David P. Norton, "Strategic Initiatives, Launching the Strategy into Motion," excerpted from "The Execution Premium: Linking Strategy to Operations for Competitive Advantage," *Harvard Business Press,* 2008, p 1.
195 Ibid.
196 Ibid.

communities in a new direction beyond the current customary policies, strategies, investments, and practices. The resulting outcome will be the stimulation of positive multipliers to have a lasting impact in these communities.

According to Klaus Schwab, founder of the World Economic Forum, we are in a world where "capital is being superseded by creativity and the ability to innovate—and therefore by human talents—as the most important factors of [global economic competitiveness]."[197] Consequently, "just as capital replaced manual trades during the process of industrialization, capital is now giving way to human talent. *Talentism is the new capitalism.*"[198]

Given the unmistakable shift toward human talent as *the* global economic differentiator in a dramatically changed and rapidly changing world, I argue that there is no greater social or economic imperative for our nation than to nurture the talent of her disconnected citizens to improve their productivity and quality of life.

THE NICCOE

Existing legislation gives the U.S. President broad executive authority to establish COEs.[199] As such, and to create a competitive economic environment throughout the whole of the nation, one of the top domestic economic policy thrusts of the U.S. President should be to establish the NICCOE.

---

197 Gary Beach, "'Talentism' Is the New Capitalism," *The Wall Street Journal, CIO Journal,* July 17, 2014, accessed November 30, 2016, http://blogs.wsj.com/cio/2014/07/17/talentism-is-the-new-capitalism/.

198 Ibid.

199 " Fact Sheet: President Obama Announces New Actions to Further Strengthen U.S. Manufacturing," The White House, Office of the Press Secretary, October 27, 2014, accessed November 30, 2016, https://www.whitehouse.gov/the-press-office/2014/10/27/fact-sheet-president-obama-announces-new-actions-further-strengthen-us-m.

Most of the $152 billion already proposed to support American Innovation in the 2017 budget is destined for projected research and development. What I propose is a total allocation of $15 billion expenditure to be budgeted over the next fifteen years. The NICCOE would annually carve out $1 billion of these funds in a strategic initiative whose primary aim would be to:

- Create COEs in urban and rural areas around the country,
- Boost Innovation Economy connectivity and productivity, and
- Improve quality of life in the nation's disconnected communities.

The proposed annual injection of $1 billion is little more than .0025 percent (that's one quarter of one thousandth of a percent) of the $4.2 trillion federal budget.[200] The investment of, say, fifteen yearly tranches is not only small in real and comparative terms but will yield excellent returns by contributing to a sustainable economic future across all demographics.

To firmly put this investment into clear perspective, consider a smaller, localized program that is currently underway in Ohio. To change the trajectory of Ohio's economy over about fifteen years, the state will invest $2.1 billion. This fund is designed to support the transformation of existing industries to a) create new, globally competitive products and b) foster the formation and attraction of new companies in emerging industry sectors.[201] As discussed in Chapter 5, this initiative is called

---

200 "What Obama wants the government to spend money on in his final presidential budget," *The Washington Post*, February 9, 2016, accessed November 30, 2016, https://www.washingtonpost.com/graphics/politics/presidential-budget-2017/.

201 "270 Companies Generated More Than $1.4 Billion in Economic Impact for Ohio in 2015 and Have Created 2,313 Direct Jobs," JumpStart Inc., July 15, 2016, accessed November 30, 2016, http://www.prnewswire.com/news-releases/270-companies-generated-more-than-14-billion-in-economic-impact-for-ohio-in-2015-and-have-created-2313-direct-jobs-300299256.html.

the Ohio Third Frontier, an internationally recognized Innovation Economy initiative.[202]

If a $2.1 billion investment, spread over fifteen years—to improve the economic productivity of a state of 11.5 million people—is reasonable, then a total national investment of $15 billion to change the economic trajectory of potentially tens of millions of disconnected Americans is not only reasonable, but eminently doable.

The NICCOE is therefore a strategic initiative with an eminently realizable goal specifically designed to catalyze and accelerate the mass of disconnected communities into action. And, once these communities gain enough momentum to achieve critical mass, then economic inclusion and competitiveness leadership, programs, and initiatives would become self-sustaining and firmly embedded into the fabric of our nation.

The NICCOE would serve as regional hubs of research, development, and deployment of economic strategies and frameworks that result in new community systems that support economic empowerment at a grassroots level. I envision a dynamic multi- and interdisciplinary NICCOE which would initially and ideally involve the:

- Department of Commerce,
- Small Business Administration,
- Department of Health and Human Services,
- National Science Foundation, and
- Department of Education.

The function of this partnership would be to coordinate leadership and services consistent with the unique attributes and capabilities of their respective organizations.

---

202 Ibid.

NATIONAL INCLUSIVE COMPETITIVENESS CENTERS OF EXCELLENCE (NICCOE)

INITIAL FEDERAL PARTNERS	MISSION
Department of Commerce's Economic Development Administration	To lead the federal economic development agenda by promoting innovation and competitiveness and preparing American regions for growth and success in the worldwide economy.
Small Business Administration	To aid, counsel, assist, and protect the interests of small business concerns, to preserve free competitive enterprise, and to maintain and strengthen the overall economy of our nation.
Department of Health and Human Services	To enhance and protect the health and well-being of all Americans by providing for effective health and human services and fostering advances in medicine, public health, and social services.
National Science Foundation	To promote the progress of science; to advance the national health, prosperity, and welfare; to secure the national defense; and for other purposes.
Department of Education	To promote student achievement and preparation for global competitiveness by fostering educational excellence and ensuring equal access.

One of the NICCOE's most important tasks is in creation and coordination of strategic public-private partnerships. Location of centers would help seed innovation and enterprise in areas of lower economic productivity. As a primary instrument of the federal government its overarching priorities would be to:

- Foster a national environment in support of economic inclusion and competitiveness.
- Significantly increase higher growth job-creating enterprises and higher impact intrapreneurial employees in economic priority areas.
- Connect community, local innovation intermediaries, philanthropic organizations, local education institutions, governments, and businesses with federal government investments in the *IC Framework*.
- Oversee and unite the national network of community systems with its overall objective of bolstering U.S. global economic competitiveness.

To this end, the NICCOE would lead the institutionalization of common performance expectations and reporting systems to further ensure that programs and strategic initiatives are linked to one another.

The NICCOE is a proposal whose main *raison d'être* is to align sectors of American society (that have been regionally or commercially isolated) with the economic sectors that already (and will in the future) offer exceptional prospects for the nation. The NICCOE would channel collaborative resources. It would act as a conduit to bring communities and forward-focused education and industry together. And it would help ensure that disconnected Americans are tightly integrated into sources of twenty-first century workforce solutions and entrepreneurial business ideas and support. It would expand the deal flow of business proposals, providing access to seed and related capital investment opportunities. It would foster visibility of and pathways to local innovation and entrepreneurship ecosystems and would coordinate comprehensive networks of services, assistance providers, and sources of financial investment.

As a nation, we need a sustainable means to counter the long-neglected issue of disempowered, disconnected communities and populations. The NICCOE would serve as a policy landmark and historic monument in the transition and transformation of the U.S. economy. It is a strong future-focused policy determined to lift the U.S. out of the enduring remnants of economic segregation toward an integrated and inclusive twenty-first century framework: one that focuses on productivity and most importantly enhances the quality of life for more Americans.

THE NICCOE MODEL

The NICCOE model represents a significant advancement in the approach of the U.S. to regional technology and innovation-based economic development, economic inclusion, and local and national competitiveness. This disruption of the existing status quo is reflected in the underlying principles of the NICCOE which include the following:

Foundations of Change

The single most critical element in the leadership and implementation of the NICCOE is how it leverages the *IC Framework* to underlie and enable policy, along with the associated investments, strategies, and practices needed to implement change. Foundationally, the NICCOE would target those individuals, institutions, and organizations that historically have not been seen as an economic priority. Its approach would embody new, multi- and interdisciplinary approaches for U.S. economic competitiveness. For the U.S. to grow and sustain national prosperity in today's Innovation Economy, we must commit to a national initiative that includes these "unusual suspects."

Achieving Impact

High-leverage engagement and intervention, based on the Trim Tab Theory discussed in Chapter 4, could enable the NICCOE to achieve its mission and deliver *more* value to disconnected Americans. The trim tab metaphor applied to the NICCOE looks like this:

- The U.S. Innovation Economy is like a **big ship** that is hard to turn,
- The **rudder** the of Innovation Economy is a nationwide network of local and regional innovation and entrepreneurship ecosystems comprised of talented people, businesses, universities, economic competitiveness and development organizations, foundations, education institutions, governments, community and human services organizations, and so on, and
- The NICCOE could act as the **trim tab.** It would exert high-leverage action to engage and turn the **rudder** (nationwide network) and, ultimately, turn the **big ship** (Innovation Economy) in the desired direction of economic inclusion and competitiveness.

Trim tab strategies will enable efficient and effective investment in new local and regional solutions that have potential for broad, perhaps even massive, impact. They allow the NICCOE to highly leverage its unique national platform and capabilities to improve the productivity and quality of life of millions of Americans.

Making Collaboration Effective

Almost all evolved and successful collaborative networks of interacting elements are enabled and nurtured by a strong hub organization or function that facilitates shared understanding, guidance, and impact.[203] The NICCOE would act in the capacity of a strong hub for national *Inclusive Competitiveness* by creating and sustaining connections with autonomous, diverse, independent, and interdependent actors.

Building Out and Scaling Up

Scaling *Inclusive Competitiveness* is fundamentally the same as scaling new enterprises. The NICCOE aims to apply a process informed by and adapted from the venture development organization JumpStart.[204] Their successful investment and intervention process was designed to build out and grow, or scale, new businesses:

- *Advise:* The NICCOE would collaborate with and provide counsel to disconnected and connected community partners to develop early, preliminary interest in potential *Inclusive Competitiveness* programs or strategic initiatives. The most promising opportunities at the local level would then be pursued.

- *Assist:* The NICCOE is designed to provide two forms of assistance to local programs or strategic initiatives: direct investment and in-kind contribution. Direct investment is defined as a monetary contribution. In-kind intervention is defined as non-monetary

---

203 Marco Iansiti and Roy Levien, , "Keystones and Dominators: Framing Operating and Technology Strategy in a Business Ecosystem," February 24, 2004, accessed September 26, 2015, http://www.keystonestrategy.com/wp-content/themes/keystone-theme/publications/pdf/Ecosystems.pdf.
204 "Program Description," GuideStar, JumpStart, Inc., accessed November 30, 2016, http://www.guidestar.org/profile/34-1398522.

and may include advisement, technical support, or funding development support.

- *Accelerate:* The NICCOE would identify the most successful *Inclusive Competitiveness* efforts. Then energy would be focused on investing additional direct and indirect resources to scale up and build out. Sustainable support for successful efforts would be sought from regional innovation and entrepreneurship ecosystems, local, state or federal governments, philanthropic or other appropriate entities, and by promoting their adoption in other areas of the U.S.

Framework for Review and Evaluation

The NICCOE initiative is a new national economic inclusion and competitiveness thrust, without the benefit of building upon historic investment or legacy of organizational and institutional infrastructure and action. A proposed framework for review and evaluation of the NICCOE might be informed by three broad categories:

- *Direct outcomes*: To measure the NICCOE's direct involvement in producing positive, on-the-ground impact in target communities. To assess the result of *Inclusive Competitiveness* policies, strategies, practices, and investments in local programs and strategic initiatives.
- *Indirect outcomes*: To measure the NICCOE's involvement to indirectly produce positive changes in the capacity of collaborative partners to address economic inclusion and competitiveness challenges in target areas. Items to assess include the use of new *Inclusive Competitiveness* policies, strategies, practices, and investments in local programs and strategic initiatives.

- *Spin-offs*: To measure the number of new *Inclusive Competitiveness* policies, strategies, and practices adopted; financial investments undertaken in programs, strategic initiatives and organizations; and mechanisms and functions created that were neither directly produced nor indirectly facilitated by the NICCOE, but that likely would not have occurred *but for* the presence of, and positive conditions fostered by, the NICCOE.

This is an especially important measure for this new national thrust. It would demonstrate that the NICCOE is successful in creating the necessary local conditions for widespread acceptance of the economic inclusion and competitiveness imperative. It would also validate—far beyond the NICCOE itself—the broad and sustained action on local and regional levels that is needed to extend *Inclusive Competitiveness* throughout the nation.

ROLES OF NICCOE PARTNERS

The model is anchored at its core by federal government partners. Initially these include the Department of Commerce, Small Business Administration, Department of Health and Human Services, National Science Foundation, and Department of Education. The term "partner" is purposefully used to connote "a collaborative relationship between entities to work toward shared objectives through a mutually agreed division of labor."[205] Each of these diverse federal departments and agencies are equipped to provide specialized focus that kindles the private sector and connects to and supports the interdisciplinary *IC Framework*.

---

205 "*Partnership for Development: Proposed Actions for the World Bank, A Discussion Paper*," *Partnerships Group, World Bank*, May 20, 1998, accessed November 30, 2016, http://www.worldbank.org/html/extdr/pfd-discpaper.pdf.

Cultivating New Economic Narratives in Disconnected Communities

The Department of Health and Human Services (DHHS) is the federal government's principal agency for providing social and human services. It covers a vast spectrum of activities that impact health, public health, and human services outcomes and protects the health and welfare of all Americans, especially for those who are least able to help themselves.[206]

Importantly, the DHHS has strong partnerships with the private sector and non-governmental organizations and leverages these resources to accomplish its mission. These vital collaborations include academic institutions, community-based nonprofit organizations, and other federal departments.[207]

The DHHS has tremendous breadth and depth, daily touching the lives of millions of Americans, many of whom are disconnected from the Innovation Economy. The DHHS could be instrumental in helping to engage local and regional human, social, and community service providers to embed a new economic narrative for people touched by the DHHS programs. Moreover, the DHHS is experienced in collaborating with and using technology platforms to reach their consumers where they are, with the information they need.[208] With the capacity to directly influence millions of Americans, the DHHS and the national human services network can be the great enablers of U.S. economic inclusion

206 U.S. Department of Health and Human Services Strategic Plan, Overview, accessed November 30, 2016, http://www.hhs.gov/about/strategic-plan/introduction/index.html#overview.

207 U.S. Department of Health and Human Services Strategic Plan, Cross-Agency Collaborations and Public-Private Partnerships, accessed November 30, 2016, http://www.hhs.gov/about/strategic-plan/introduction/index.html#collaborations.

208 "U.S. Department of Health and Human Services, Department of Health and Human Services collaborates with top technology platforms to reach consumers about the Health Insurance Marketplace," December 17, 2014, accessed November 30, 2016, http://www.hhs.gov/about/news/2014/12/17/department-health-and-human-services-collaborates-with-top-technology-platforms-to-reach-consumers-about-the-health-insurance-marketplace.html.

and competitiveness. They can be the force multiplier of the NICCOE, dramatically increasing its reach and effectiveness.

The nation's human services sector generally has not been involved with U.S. innovation and economic competitiveness leadership and action. Engaging them around the *IC Framework* would be a crucial first step in nurturing new economic narratives in disconnected communities, which are an essential asset to building a resilient, inclusive national economy.

Evolving STEM to STEAM to Power Employment and Entrepreneurship in Disconnected Communities

It's a well-accepted notion that improving U.S. economic competitiveness requires a vast increase in the number of Americans with high levels of proficiency and expertise in STEM. In fact, STEM is already a national education and economic priority. The Department of Education (DOE) has current programs designed to:

- Facilitate a cohesive national strategy to increase the impact of federal investments in improving STEM instruction in preschool through twelfth grade,
- Increase and sustain public and youth engagement with STEM,
- Improve the STEM experience for undergraduate students,
- Better serve groups historically underrepresented in STEM fields, and
- Design graduate education for tomorrow's STEM workforce.[209]

Undeniably, STEM disciplines gird a disproportionately large number of job-creating HGEs, enable enormous efficiency and produc-

---

209 U.S. Department of Education Science, Technology, Engineering and Math: Education for Global Leadership, accessed November 30, 2016, http://www.ed.gov/stem.

tivity gains in existing industries, and represent many of our top employment opportunities. However, as important as STEM is to our economy, a focus on it alone is too limiting. It will be insufficient to generate enough American innovators to create the companies and fill the jobs we're counting on to power U.S. economic prosperity. And it will be particularly limiting in terms of driving *inclusive* economic growth and innovation.

Higher growth entrepreneurship and higher impact employment are fueled by more than just science. They are also fueled by art. The DOE must ensure that the NICCOE incorporates the "A" for art and evolves STEM to STEAM.

The Innovation Economy demands new education and entrepreneurship models and interdisciplinary solutions that combine imagination and creativity with technological skills. There is growing recognition that to be successful in technical fields, individuals must also be creative. They need to use critical thinking skills and contextual understanding of enterprise development that are nurtured through exposure to the arts, including design, media, sociology, psychology, and history. If the role that art plays in entrepreneurship and employment is de-emphasized and undervalued, it will isolate certain segments of the population from a growing amount of technology-based, change-making, and problem-solving opportunities.

Simply put, the NICCOE should reject the increasingly, if not definitively, false choice between "soft art" or "hard science." To improve entrepreneurship and employment outcomes for disconnected Americans we need to integrate art into the equation: it must be STEAM, not STEM.

The abilities to work collaboratively across many disciplines, challenge current practice, and develop new solutions and opportunities—attributes which are clearly more art than science—are highly desired skills. In fact, an IBM global study of more than 1,500 CEOs from sixty countries and thirty-three industries concerning twenty-first century employment found that the most important skill needed to successfully navigate an increasingly complex, volatile, and uncertain world is *creativity*.[210]

Art is also vital to HGE and job creation. STEM does indeed create a considerable amount of the intellectual property (IP) produced by innovators and researchers, and builds skills needed to drive Innovation Economy priorities. However, by introducing creative market applications, art makes such IP and skills useful across a broader spectrum of our economy, achieving greater positive impact.

By moving STEM-based IP from the laboratories, workshops in our basements, garages, colleges, universities, and corporations and into markets where they have the most impact, STEAM is the market application force for STEM. Design, marketing and communication, executive leadership, collaboration, and technology transfer are just a few of the many skills which find their roots in art and creativity; the ingredients needed to translate technological innovations into thriving businesses.

The DOE can lead the national shift from STEM to STEAM, bolstering efforts to construct new, inclusive narratives and action around entrepreneurship, innovation, employment, and economic competitiveness. The DOE's partnership with the NICCOE and adoption of STEAM gives the nation a chance to fully engage a diverse array of talent who can be the innovative, job-creating entrepreneurs and top-performing employees our economy badly needs.

---

210 Steven Tepper, "Is An MFA The New MBA?" Fast Company, March 38, 2013, accessed November 30, 2016, http://www.fastcompany.com/3007541/mfa-new-mba.

Creating Innovation and Competitiveness Organizations in Disconnected Communities

The Department of Commerce's EDA is the only federal government agency focused exclusively on economic development. It leads the federal government's economic development agenda by promoting innovation and competitiveness that prepares American regions for growth and success in the worldwide economy.[211] The EDA plays a critical role in fostering regional economic development efforts in communities across the nation, making strategic investments that foster job creation and support development in economically distressed areas of the U.S.[212]

Advancing economic inclusion and competitiveness in disconnected communities requires identifying opportunities that can also enhance productivity along existing local and regional economic priorities and objectives. A primary, but not exclusive, expression of these priorities and objectives is codified as the area's Comprehensive Economic Development Strategy (CEDS). The purpose of the CEDS is to analyze the regional economy and serve as a guide to establish regional goals and objectives, develop and implement a regional plan of action, and identify investment priorities and funding sources.[213] A strategic planning process and important tool of the CEDS is to bring together the public and private sectors in the creation of an economic road-mapping document to diversify and strengthen regional economies. Critically important is that federal law requires a CEDS in order for a community to apply for and win investment assistance from the EDA.[214]

---

211 "About EDA," U.S. Department of Commerce Economic Development Administration, accessed November 30, 2016, https://www.eda.gov/about/.

212 Ibid.

213 "Summary of Requirements," U.S. Department of Commerce, Economic Development Administration, Comprehensive Economic Development Strategies (CEDS), accessed November 30, 2016, https://www.eda.gov/pdf/CEDS_Flyer_Wht_Backround.pdf.

214 Ibid.

The CEDS, as well as other areas of promising economic opportunity, can serve as a guiding North Star for economic inclusion and competitiveness, articulating where the community is heading and informing how disconnected Americans can connect to where it is going. Additionally, the EDA helps create the conditions for economic growth by:

- Leveraging regional focus and national programs,
- Investing in ecosystem builders,
- Building capacity and reinforcing the culture of innovation, and
- Encouraging and supporting public-private partnerships.[215]

These approaches align with the *IC Framework*. They can help create new community systems and organizations focused on economic inclusion and competitiveness that support the following desirable outcomes:

- Creation, facilitation, and monitoring of singular and collaborative actions among key actors, such as economic competitiveness organizations; social, human, and education service organizations; minority-serving professional associations and organizations; and schools and education systems designed to create and fill jobs.
- Working with partners to apply and enhance proven tech- and innovation-based economic development principles, practices, and strategies to increase intrapreneurial employment prospects and job-creating entrepreneurship performance.

---

215 "The Regional Innovation Strategies Program," Economic Development Administration Office of Innovation and Entrepreneurship, May 17, 2016, accessed November 30, 2016, https://www.eda.gov/oie/files/ris/20160518-RIS-Hill-Briefing.pdf.

- Connecting and convening public, private, and academic partners to inform the vision, strategy, and priorities for inclusively increasing economic competitiveness.
- Collaboration with and monitoring for funding opportunities. These include local, state, federal, and regional government sources and regional, national, and corporate philanthropy.
- Collecting and communicating economic inclusion and competitiveness performance data for partners and preparing strategy presentations and position papers for broad dissemination.

The EDA is uniquely positioned to fund and enable meaningful programs and strategic initiatives. These are capable of catalyzing a national movement to advance economic inclusion and competitiveness. The NICCOE can be most effective if it has deep involvement and alignment with the EDA, which is essential to command national respect and marshal local and federal resources to meet these objectives.

Creating Clusters that Benefit Disconnected Communities

The U.S. Small Business Administration (SBA) invests in regional innovation clusters throughout the nation that span a variety of industries.[216] Clusters are geographic concentrations of interconnected companies, specialized suppliers, academic institutions, service providers, and associated organizations with a specific industry focus.[217] For example, the following diagram shows an anatomy of the biopharmaceuticals cluster in Boston, MA.[218]

---

216 "About the SBA: Clusters Initiative," U.S. Small Business Administration, accessed November 30, 2016, https://www.sba.gov/about-sba/sba-initiatives/clusters-initiative.
217 Ibid.
218 "U.S. Cluster Mapping Project 2014," U.S. Department of Commerce, accessed November 30, 2016, http://www.clustermapping.us/content/clusters-101.

THE BOSTON BIOPHARMACEUTICALS CLUSTER

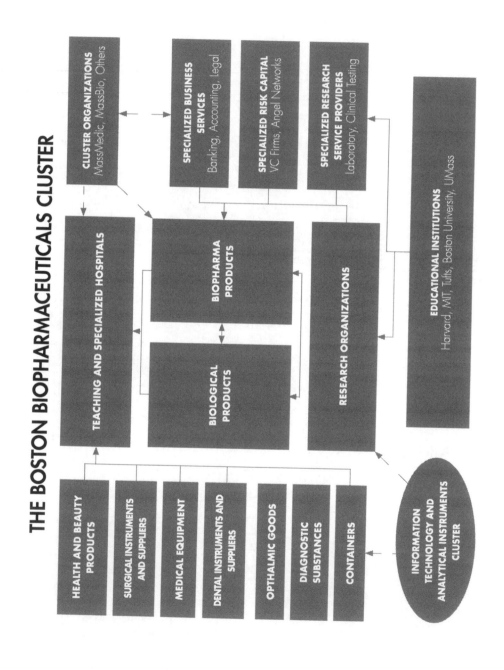

Clusters are flexible, adaptable, and broadly applicable and have the potential to help create more globally competitive cities and regions. They are the most effective and efficient tool by which to organize collaborative and actionable economic competitiveness leadership.[219] By aligning assets and creating shared strategies for competitiveness and growth, states, regions, and cities across the U.S. are able to optimize the use of existing resources. This allows for strategic investment in programs and infrastructure that can benefit all cluster actors, including entrepreneurs, workers, investors, educators, businesses, and support organizations. Infusing economic inclusion and competitiveness into these same clusters can also improve overall performance and has the potential to help disconnected communities become proverbial hubs-of-the-wheels of local and regional economic prosperity instead of the holes-in-doughnuts.[220]

Figure 1. ScaleUp Partners' Model for Improving U.S. Global Economic Competitiveness by Infusing Innovation Clusters with Inclusive Competitiveness

The illustration above shows how innovation cluster policy and practice can be infused with *Inclusive Competitiveness* and ultimately make for healthier national and global economies by boosting the productivity of local and regional economies.

Building clusters that embrace disconnected Americans is a foundation upon which improved national competitiveness can be achieved. Yet, like other areas of the Innovation Economy described in

219 Johnathan M. Holifield, Adam Kamins, and Teresa M. Lynch, "Inclusive Clusters,"*Economic Development Journal*, Fall 2012, Volume 11, Number 4, accessed November 30, 2016, http://masseconomics.com/wp-content/uploads/2014/05/EDJ_12_Fall_InclusiveClusters.pdf.

220 Ibid.

this book, cluster policy and practice are implemented by connected actors who typically overlook disconnected communities. As a result, these communities are unable to fulfill their economic potential largely due to two key reasons. First, the benefits associated with cluster-based economic development bypass those with the greatest need. And second, the ability of cluster policies and practices to efficiently unleash growth is hindered. This is because the unique and untapped advantages associated with disconnected communities—such as transportation nodes, education and cultural entities, proximity to market-leading economic assets, and large numbers of potential customers—are not capitalized upon.

Without an appropriate emphasis on economic inclusion and competitiveness in the cluster exploration and selection phases, the *Inclusive Competitiveness* challenges associated with cluster-based strategies can become nearly insurmountable. Therefore, an important first step in any cluster-based approach involves choosing clusters that promote widespread growth in different and diverse parts of a city or region, including its disconnected communities.

Additionally, while targeting higher growth clusters is acceptable and necessary, the full set of target clusters cannot be limited to only those that create job opportunities for the most highly educated workers. This can be avoided by considering one or more of the following during the cluster exploration, selection, and prioritization phases:

- Education and training requirements, to ensure that barriers to cluster entry are not prohibitive,
- The distribution of cluster jobs and wages, as the ideal targets could promote opportunities for middle-wage jobs and advancement for populations without college degrees,

- The geography of cluster activities, to ensure that not only regional but inner city and other disconnected area strengths are being targeted, and

- The capital requirements needed and availability of investment mechanisms for new enterprises. Emphasis would be on clusters that create opportunities for entrepreneurs without access to high levels of personal or "friends and family" wealth.[221]

The SBA—in its local and regional cluster exploration and selection process—should incorporate these approaches, which reflect an understanding of the demography and geography of opportunity associated with employment and entrepreneurship. Put another way, people and businesses with strong existing, yet detached, networks that could advance the target clusters and support new economic activity provide another key lever when it comes to improving economic productivity and quality of life in disconnected communities. As such, the NICCOE can be a tool through which SBA can facilitate demographic and geographic expansion of economic competitiveness through wide-ranging and inclusive cluster exploration and selection to benefit the target communities.

Applying Innovation and Entrepreneurship Ecosystem Policies, Practices and Expectations in Disconnected Communities

The National Science Foundation (NSF) is an independent federal agency created by Congress in 1950 "to promote the progress of science; to advance the national health, prosperity, and welfare; to secure the national defense ... "[222] Today, the NSF is an innovation powerhouse and

---

221 Ibid.
222 "NSA At-A-Glance," National Science Foundation, accessed November 30, 2016, http://www.nsf.gov/about/glance.jsp.

one of the nation's leading sources of innovation investment! It is the funding source for approximately 24 percent of all federally supported basic research conducted by America's colleges and universities and is a major source of federal backing in other fields such as mathematics, computer science, and the social sciences.[223] Significantly, the NSF's enabling legislation authorizes it to support activities designed to increase the participation of women and minorities and others underrepresented in science and technology.[224] This is the purpose to which the NICCOE can connect to bring the NSF into the national strategy to improve the economic competitiveness and quality of life of disconnected Americans.

The NSF is also a national leader for fostering and promoting local and regional innovation and entrepreneurship ecosystems. A key component of the NSF's stewardship of these ecosystems is that the agency aspires to instil an understanding of innovation[225] through sponsored research to improve the hard data for innovation policy.[226] Embracing risk-astute investment strategies through its sponsored research grants, the NSF's leadership is designed to penetrate deeply and broadly across the country,[227] including effecting positive impact on disconnected communities that need exactly what the NSF is chartered to deliver. There is clear alignment of disconnected communities' needs and the provision of solutions through the NSF.

The collaborative mechanism the NSF deploys to build, utilize, and sustain the national innovation and entrepreneurship ecosystem is the

---

223 Ibid.
224 Ibid.
225 Ibid.
226 "Expanding Understanding of the Innovation Process: R&D and Non-R&D Innovation," National Science Foundation Award Abstract #1262418, 2013, accessed November 30, 2016, http://www.nsf.gov/awardsearch/showAward?AWD_ID=1262418.
227 "NSF Vision of the Innovation Ecosystem," National Science Foundation, Innovation Corps, accessed November 30, 2016, https://www.nsf.gov/news/special_reports/i-corps/ecosystem.jsp.

National Innovation Network (NIN), which cultivates the understanding of how to:

- Identify, develop, and support promising ideas that can generate value,
- Create and implement tools and resources that enhance our nation's innovation capacity,
- Gather, analyze, evaluate, and utilize the data and insight resulting from the experiences of those participating in NSF programs; these programs foster entrepreneurship that can lead to the commercialization of technology that has been supported previously by NSF-funded research, and
- Share and leverage effective innovation practices on a national scale to improve the quality of life for all Americans.[228]

The NIN catalyzes local teams to explore the transition of technology concepts into the marketplace. It offers infrastructure, resources, and networking opportunities to serve the teams and to develop local ecosystems. These in turn contribute to a larger, national network of mentors, researchers, entrepreneurs, and investors.

The NSF must also undertake to "promote the progress of science" and advance local innovation and entrepreneurship ecosystems in disconnected communities. Application of these policies and practices in these communities can help create a new environment and conditions that encourage economic inclusion and competitiveness.

As detailed in Chapter 2, disconnected communities are served by a rich and diverse set of education and economic nonprofit organizations. Acting together, the NSF and NICCOE would complement existing leadership and services with new infrastructure and strategies. Their

---

228 Ibid.

combined focus on creating new ecosystems to link disconnected Americans to the Innovation Economy could lead to these Americans producing a larger share of future national economic, business, employment, and income growth. This infrastructure and strategy, supported by related local institutions and organizations, can make new economic narratives real and tangible. The result will be seen in new and flourishing economic opportunities and a larger pipeline of talent that can become economic athletes, i.e., job-creating entrepreneurs and high-performing employees.

Launching *Inclusive Competitiveness* on a national scale will require the NICCOE to advance new policies and practices across a diverse set of public and private stakeholders. These include business organizations and anti-poverty groups, as well as the academic, research, corporate, and philanthropic communities. Equally, disconnected communities also need funders and investors to increase risk-tolerance and adopt the same levels of expectation in their communities as exist in local and regional innovation and economic competitiveness efforts. This can be achieved by adopting innovation and competitiveness investment strategies and funding approaches consistent with thoughtful risk-taking philosophies, such as those employed by the EDA and NSF.

It is essential to move beyond the existing paradigms to create change and encourage growth and development in our nation's disconnected communities. New funding needs to be deployed within a more relaxed and fully accountable framework. This will allow for needed experimentation which will tie the funding to projects that demonstrate broad economic inclusion and competitiveness and are open to subsequent evaluation and broad dissemination of their findings. This level of investigation, risk tolerance, and communication is critical for the sustained implementation and ongoing success of the *IC Framework.*

CHAPTER 10

CALL TO A NATIONAL MOVEMENT

---

*I*nclusive Competitiveness is aligned with and reflects the zeit-geist—the defining spirit, ideas, and mood of the times in which we live. These synergistic elements create the unique opportunity for the nation to pursue an agenda of shared prosperity. The futurist Alvin Toffler said, "The illiterate of the 21st century will not be those who cannot read and write, but those who cannot learn, unlearn, and relearn." In this moment, disconnected Americans and the policymaking class are called to ignite a National *Inclusive Competitiveness* Movement to spread twenty-first century literacy. And there is no greater time to act than the present.

As I mentioned in the Introduction, "disconnected communities and individuals simply have not been *offered* [Innovation Economy] opportunities—nor have they *demanded* them ... now is the time for disconnected communities to meet new economic *offerings* by not just wishing for, but *demanding* a piece of the innovation pie!"

A June 2015 poll published in the *New York Times* and CBS News found that most Americans believe that just a few people at the top have a chance to get ahead and that the money and wealth in this country should be more evenly distributed.[229] Promisingly, these opinions spread the breadth of the political gamut: the vast majority of Democrats and most independents say wealth should be more evenly distributed, and Republicans are closely split.[230] Perhaps no time in the past forty years has been riper than now to adopt a serious policy regime to *offer* new pathways to all Americans, especially the disconnected, to satisfy their new *demand* to access the nation's best opportunities.

NEED ALL HANDS ON DECK

The disquiet of the nation is a sign to America's policymaking influencers to advocate and activate new policies that will ignite and sustain a National *Inclusive Competitiveness* Movement. Essentially, this is a call for an *All Hands on Deck* leadership thrust that would have but one goal: to ensure that every American has a fair opportunity to compete and succeed in the Innovation Economy and improve their quality of life.

Presently, all American hands are not on board. We are not all able to seize twenty-first century opportunities. We are not all exploring new innovations and raising the nation's competitive position. This is a recipe for fleeting, episodic, and narrow prosperity, not of the broad and enduring nature needed.

As this book details, the mature practices of the current national network of regional innovation and entrepreneurship ecosystems, which undergird the Innovation Economy, have had little impact on

---

229 "Americans' Views on Income Inequality and Workers' Rights," *The New York Times-CBS News* Poll, June 3, 2015, accessed November 30, 2016, http://www.nytimes.com/interactive/2015/06/03/business/income-inequality-workers-rights-international-trade-poll.html?_r=3.
230 Ibid.

disconnected communities. These Americans have experienced a record of negligible cultivation and minimal engagement. To best serve these communities, a new national policy regime focused on economic inclusion and competitiveness must be adopted. New capacities and capabilities must be developed for the U.S. to access the heretofore untapped talents of more Americans. Now is the time for disconnected Americans to press policymaking influencers hard throughout the U.S.–and for those already connected to the Innovation Economy to join with them–to pursue a new course: *All Hands on Deck* policy to activate a National *Inclusive Competitiveness* Movement.

NO WHITE HORSE FOR DISCONNECTED AMERICANS

My mother said something several years ago that has stayed with me ever since. I had been complaining about an especially difficult problem I was confronting. While I was not responsible for creating the situation, the responsibility for solving it rested squarely on my shoulders and resolution required significant assistance from others. At my wits end, in exasperation, I said to her, "Man, oh man, I really need someone to come along on a white horse to save the day."

Without missing a beat, my mother quipped, "Johnny, I've got news for you: the person who's coming on a white horse is coming to tell you that no one's coming to your rescue."

It was like a cold splash of water to my face! I paused, thought for a second, chuckled a bit, then said with complete resignation and acceptance, "Yeah, Ma, you're right. No one's coming to my rescue."

This was what I call a White Horse Moment: the moment when you realize that while you may not be the singular cause of your current predicament, you do bear the *initial responsibility* and *final accountability* for getting out of that predicament. While help may be needed, requested, welcomed, or accepted along the way, you do what it takes to resolve the predicament and take charge of the final outcome.

And so it is for disconnected Americans: if we are to see the creation of a National *Inclusive Competitiveness* Movement then this will not happen without those in need taking responsibility and stepping up to demand change to steer themselves toward better opportunities and a brighter future.

Certainly, no thinking person believes that disconnected communities are solely liable for their economic predicament. Often the environment is a result of passive acceptance of the current status quo. In other respects, the challenges they face are the result of global restructuring, ineffective national policies, and historic discriminatory economic practices. However, disconnected Americans carry the *initial responsibility* and *final accountability* for righting their economic ship. And if they don't immediately get into this game, then they risk being irretrievably left in an uncompetitive and insufficiently productive twentieth century paradigm.

For sure, as discussed throughout this book, these Americans need help. In my experience, the needed help will be drawn to disconnected communities that *initiate* new demands to access the nation's best opportunities while undertaking new actions that are aligned with improving their competitiveness and productivity. The help provided can assist these communities on the journey to their *final* destination or endgame: improved quality of life.

POLICYMAKERS: CAST DOWN YOUR BUCKET WHERE YOU ARE

As this book expresses, it is incumbent upon influential policymakers throughout the U.S. to provide leadership to foster conditions conducive for a National *Inclusive Competitiveness* Movement. This can be the beginning of intentionally *offering* disconnected Americans new community systems to help them access Innovation Economy opportunities. Policymakers across the diverse spectrum of business, government, philanthropic, and civic leadership should note that *Inclusive Competitiveness* is politically, socially, and economically agnostic. It owes allegiance to no particular philosophy or ideology. Its fidelity is solely to the objective of improving the productivity and quality of life of disconnected Americans and their communities.

Regrettably, to meet the nation's workforce and business creation needs, many in the policymaking class have chosen to expend huge amounts of financial, political, and social capital on the issue of attracting foreign talent to the U.S. without giving much consideration to improving the economic competitiveness of disconnected Americans. The H1B non-immigrant visa, for example, allows U.S. companies to employ foreign workers in specialty occupations that require theoretical or technical expertise in specialized fields such as architecture, engineering, mathematics, science, and medicine. The prevalent use of these visas has become quite contentious as it appears to have an adverse effect on the hiring of disconnected Americans.[231]

My belief is that exclusively focusing on either immigrant *or* disconnected American talent is a false and destructive choice. I certainly

---

231 Deepak Chitnis, "Hiring workers on H-1B visas equals to less women, minorities in Silicon Valley offices," *The American Bazar,* April 30, 2014, accessed November 30, 2016, http://www.americanbazaaronline.com/2014/04/30/hiring-workers-h-1b-visas-equals-less-women-minorities-silicon-valley-offices/.

recognize the value of attracting talent from around the world to the U.S. In reality, there are only two ways to improve America's talent pool:

1. Attract more of it from outside the country, and
2. Develop and empower more of it from within the country.

Accordingly, the prudent course is to pursue the path that equitably addresses both concerns.

Here's the game-changing point: the global race for talent, in which growing numbers of nations are competing, has led to the inability of any single nation to recruit its way to sustained prosperity. There are simply far too many nations going after the world's "best and brightest." At most, global talent attraction can be the "icing on a cake"– something sweet, enhancing, and complementary–where the incumbent population itself is the cake.

At the end of the day, for the U.S. to grow enough talent to meet the employment and entrepreneurship needs of a world-leading economy, we must look within the nation and to disconnected Americans. For guidance, U.S. policymakers can revisit the poignant instruction provided by a former slave who rose up from that wretched condition to build one of the nation's great universities,[232] Booker T. Washington.

Today, it's important for the policymaking class to look back and reflect on Washington's instruction from over 120 years ago, which still has potency and the power to inform an inclusive approach to building a more resilient and competitive national economy. It is cloaked in a fable and excerpted from his historic September 18, 1895 speech at the International Exposition in Atlanta, Georgia:

> A ship lost at sea for many days suddenly sighted a
> friendly vessel. From the mast of the unfortunate vessel

---

232 Tuskegee University.

was seen a signal, "Water, water; we die of thirst!" The answer from the friendly vessel at once came back, "Cast down your bucket where you are." A second time the signal, "Water, water; send us water!" ran up from the distressed vessel, and was answered, "Cast down your bucket where you are." And a third and fourth signal for water was answered, "Cast down your bucket where you are." The captain of the distressed vessel, at last heeding the injunction, cast down his bucket, and it came up full of fresh, sparkling water from the mouth of the Amazon River.

For our purposes, the moral of Washington's fable is that the policymaking class should cast down its bucket where it is, in the U.S., particularly in disconnected communities, and empower all Americans to contribute their full potential to improve the economic competitiveness of the nation and their own quality of life.

In times of great distress and enormous challenges—which we are certainly experiencing today—instead of looking out onto the world horizon for economic salvation, policymakers should look first to those assets and resources that can be accessed and activated from within their own country and communities and *offer* them a fair chance at the nation's top opportunities. Policymakers: cast down your bucket right here, right now.

Failure to move toward shared prosperity may result in nothing less than destabilizing our democratic system and rendering its exalted ideals impotent. Through a National *Inclusive Competitiveness* Movement, we can do much more as a nation to intentionally position all of our people to become economic athletes and contributors to America's next generation of vitality and global competitiveness. Endowed with the unalienable right of choice—the thing that distinguishes the great American experiment from every other in the world—there is absolutely nothing stopping us from choosing to pursue the path of national economic mobility and security across our demographic and geographic divides. We can no longer stand by and expect others to act for us. For meaningful change we need to act individually and collectively. Such change can only occur when we take responsibility and build the necessary public will to kindle the National *Inclusive Competitiveness* Movement.

AN INVITATION FROM SCALEUP PARTNERS

Now more than ever, more and more communities are beginning to realize that to play a meaningful part in the future of our nation while improving opportunities and quality of life for all, they must become part of the twenty-first century tech-driven, globally competitive economy.

At ScaleUp Partners, our singular focus is to help ignite the National *Inclusive Competitiveness* Movement at local, regional, and national levels. Whether you want to define your first step or are further along in the process, we invite you to reach out to us to continue this dialogue.

Our national network of culturally competent bilingual economic strategists speaks the dual languages of twentieth century obsolescence and twenty-first century innovation. Our primary purpose is to help build socioeconomic bridges to and from the Innovation Economy. We show disconnected communities and policymakers how to develop policies, strategies, and practices that can shift stubbornly stagnant metrics to achieve shared success.

We understand the challenges local leaders face: putting effective strategies into action and identifying both the myriad sources of untapped potential and the resources needed to achieve multi-faceted goals.

When you partner with ScaleUp Partners, you will benefit from our proprietary methods developed from years of experience working with communities of all sizes and economic conditions.

We are deeply passionate about and committed to helping cities, regions, and states cultivate new outcomes—outcomes that disrupt the inertia of declining or non-existent economic productivity while at the same time helping unlock the value hidden in communities by connecting them to the Innovation Economy.

To discover how we can benefit you, your organization, and your community, visit us at www.ScaleUpPartners.com.

A SPECIAL THANK YOU TO MY SPONSORS

 KAPOR CENTER
FOR SOCIAL IMPACT

LEADING TECH
INTO THE FUTURE

America's first frontier was the agricultural economy; the second frontier was the industrial age, and the third frontier is today's tech-driven economy. The fourth frontier will be creating an inclusive Innovation Economy, which is all about creating new community systems to improve economic productivity and quality of life in disconnected communities. One of the greatest examples of an organization leading the way to infuse and grow our economy with diverse talent is the Kapor Center for Social Impact.

The Kapor (pronounced KAY-por) Center has long recognized that Silicon Valley and the national tech economy have lacked diversity and have missed out on the enormous value that inclusive and competitive talent can contribute. Over the years, and now from its purposefully conspicuous presence in Oakland, CA, the Kapor Center has acted on this recognition, making groundbreaking contributions to diversify America's technology and entrepreneurship ecosystems. Not only does the Kapor Center provide keen insights from successful business ventures—stretching as far back as the founding of Lotus Development

Corporation and designing Lotus 1-2-3–it also leverages deep professional experience in research and nonprofit initiatives on addressing implicit bias, fostering diversity, and advocating for full inclusion.

During the first White House Tech Inclusion Summit (of which they were the driving force) and the inaugural UNCF Historically Black Colleges and Universities Innovation Summit (of which they were the primary sponsor), I had the privilege to meet and observe the "tech power couple" and founders of the Kapor Center, Mitch Kapor and Freada Kapor Klein. I was instantly taken by their profound commitment, openness, and generosity. It's easy for me to admire the Kapors. Our values are aligned. We both "believe that when the community of tech leaders reflects the diversity of the United States, tech will play an integral role in closing gaps and disparities that exist in this country," as they say–making us stronger, together.

By bringing to bear this unique blend of vision and assets on its particular area of interest, disconnected communities "that have historically been on the periphery of access to opportunity, participation and influence in the United States," the Kapor Center is distinguished as a one-of-a-kind American enterprise advancing *Inclusive Competitiveness* throughout the nation.

Contact them at:

Kapor Center for Social Impact

2148 Broadway

Oakland, CA 94612

www.kaporcenter.org

@kaporcenter

ADVANCING ECONOMIC INCLUSION
AND COMPETITIVENESS "FOR OTHERS"

Based on more than 450 years of Jesuit educational tradition, at the core of John Carroll University (JCU) are transcendent values, which include a commitment to building a more just world. The embodiment of this value was perfectly expressed in 1973 by Father Pedro Arrupe, S.J., Superior General of the Society of Jesus, who employed the phrase "Men for Others" to provocatively challenge the alumni of Jesuit schools and universities to be engaged in the struggle for justice to protect the needs of the most vulnerable. As more Jesuit schools became co-ed, this was expanded to "Men and Women for Others."

I am honored that JCU president, Rev. Robert L. Niehoff, S.J., recognizes that *Inclusive Competitiveness* carries the spirit of "Men and Women for Others" forward into our economy. He correctly notes that *Inclusive Competitiveness* involves bringing innovation, employment, entrepreneurship, and twenty-first century economic opportunities to others—where they are—with our neighbors in their neighborhoods to help improve quality of life.

Fr. Niehoff, a Jesuit-educated scholar, businessman, and veteran academic leader, understands that poor and deteriorating economic conditions can hinder neighborhood access to opportunities and thwart our neighbors' efforts to become all they are ordained to be. These communities generally are isolated from the Innovation Economy, including education services and opportunities aligned with today's top economic sectors, new jobs, idea-nurturing business incubators and accelerators, and more.

A JCU education prepares students for the journey to discover who the world needs them to become, with the expectation that they actively engage to improve conditions and help remove barriers to our nation's best education and economic opportunities. *Inclusive Competitiveness* and the *IC Framework* are practical approaches for students desiring to manifest the Jesuit mission and their preparation into meaningful action with and "for Others."

JCU is located in University Heights, Ohio, a suburban community in The Heights, just east of the city of Cleveland. It is one of the twenty-eight private, co-educational Jesuit Catholic universities in the United States.

Contact them at:

John Carroll University

1 John Carroll Blvd

University Heights, OH 44118

www.jcu.edu

@JohnCarrollU

GLOSSARY OF KEY LEADERSHIP CONCEPTS AND TERMS OF INCLUSIVE COMPETITIVENESS

A.O.L.: Aggregate, Organize, and Leverage

Collaborative, three-step process for community leaders to bring clarity to engaging unwieldy problems:

- **A**ggregate local leadership, wealth, and resources
- **O**rganize the aggregated local leadership, wealth, and resources into useful and actionable forms, and
- **L**everage the aggregated and organized local leadership, wealth, and resources to implement collaborative, high-impact programs, projects, and initiatives that further community goals.

Connected Citizens

Citizens with the awareness, competencies, and contacts to successfully perform within innovation and entrepreneurship ecosystems and clusters, emerging industry sectors, and other areas critical to national economic competitiveness. The term is used to distinguish from disconnected citizens (below).

Diagnosis

Informed by the practice of medicine, diagnosis is the process through which disconnected and connected communities can jointly identify and assess the causes of conditions that undermine economic productivity and quality of life in the Innovation Economy. The term is used in combination with discovery (below).

Disconnected Citizens

Citizens without the awareness, competencies, and contacts to successfully perform within innovation and entrepreneurship ecosystems and clusters, emerging industry sectors, and other areas critical to national economic competitiveness. The term is used to distinguish from connected citizens (above).

Discovery

Informed by the practice of law, discovery is the process through which disconnected and connected communities can jointly uncover solutions and develop strategies to address the causes of conditions that undermine economic productivity and quality of life in the Innovation Economy. The term is used in combination with diagnosis (above).

Economic Athletes

Individuals who demonstrate the skills mastery, creativity, agility, grit, and stamina to achieve sustained economic mobility, security, and prosperity, as well as life satisfaction.

Economic Empowerment

People and communities that have the capacity to bring about a sustainable state of economic growth, development, and competitiveness rooted in education, entrepreneurship, employment, and capital formation and investment.

Eight Communities of Influence

As defined by Mike Green, Co-founder of ScaleUp Partners, these are key roles within a community that can exert meaningful influence on local Innovation Economy priorities and activities. They include Education, Development, Industry, Entrepreneurship, Funding, Policy, Community, and Communications. (See page 207 for the Eight Communities of Influence framework.)

Equity Citizens

Informed by the equity partner concept in business, equity citizens are full and equal citizens under law by either birthright or acquisition through naturalization or other legal means. Equity citizens are entitled and able to access an equitable proportion of their country's best opportunities and hold underlying economic ownership, wealth, or other interests in their nation. The term is used to distinguish from non-equity citizens (below).

Inclusive Competitiveness

Policies, strategies, practices, and metrics to create community systems to improve the productivity and quality of life of disconnected populations and communities in the Innovation Economy. Importantly, *Inclusive Competitiveness* neither alters nor replaces, but rather complements and enhances, existing and emerging local, regional, state, and national economic competitiveness strategies and metrics with an exclusive focus on the productivity of disconnected populations and communities.

Inclusive Competitiveness Diffusion

Diffusion is the process by which innovations spread within and across economies. Diffusion of *Inclusive Competitiveness* within regional innovation and entrepreneurship ecosystems and clusters helps make them more productive. Increased productivity of these regional ecosystems and clusters creates more economically competitive regional economies, leading to more economically competitive state, national, and global economies.

These results are achieved by empowering disconnected citizens to become the connected citizens who create and seize new opportunities that improve the productivity of these ecosystems and clusters, leading to better overall economic performance. (See page 273 for Inclusive Competitiveness diffusion model.)

Inclusive Competitiveness Framework

A model illustrating the key components, interdependent strategies, and outcomes that can be used by communities to improve the productivity of disconnected populations and communities. (See pages 81 and 199 for IC Framework model.)

Inclusive Competitiveness Pillars

Inclusive Competitiveness consists of five pillars:

1. Policy enabling, which takes place in both the public and private sector,
2. Education attainment, specifically STEAM (science, technology, engineering, art, and math),
3. Entrepreneurship, principally higher growth,
4. Employment, particularly higher impact, and
5. Risk capital formation and investment, including public, private, equity, debt, and credit.

ScaleUp Partners' Model for Diffusing Inclusive Competitiveness

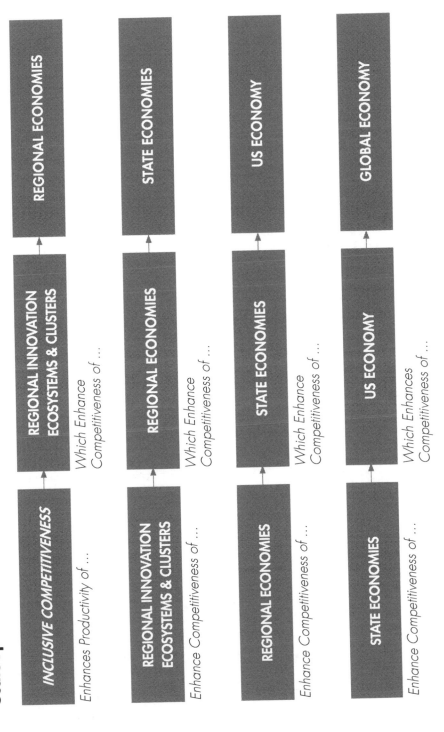

INCLUSIVE COMPETITIVENESS

Enhances Productivity of ...

REGIONAL INNOVATION ECOSYSTEMS & CLUSTERS

Which Enhance Competitiveness of ...

REGIONAL ECONOMIES

REGIONAL INNOVATION ECOSYSTEMS & CLUSTERS

Enhance Competitiveness of ...

REGIONAL ECONOMIES

Which Enhance Competitiveness of ...

STATE ECONOMIES

REGIONAL ECONOMIES

Enhance Competitiveness of ...

STATE ECONOMIES

Which Enhance Competitiveness of ...

US ECONOMY

STATE ECONOMIES

Enhance Competitiveness of ...

US ECONOMY

Which Enhances Competitiveness of ...

GLOBAL ECONOMY

Innovation Economy

The period in the late twentieth and early twenty-first centuries marked by profound socioeconomic changes brought about by convergence of globalized commerce, democratized information and technology, accelerated new knowledge creation, exponential entrepreneurship growth, and interconnectedness of the world.

Innovation Economy Squeeze

Refers to the increasing pressure on workers due to business efficiency gains from new technology adoption (i.e., automation) and global competition for jobs.

Innovation and Entrepreneurship Ecosystem

Like the natural world, everything in the Innovation Economy is connected. An innovation and entrepreneurship ecosystem is an interconnected, interdependent, and balanced community of assets, including:

- People and talent (entrepreneurs/management),
- Capital (equity/credit/debt),
- Organizations (innovation intermediaries),
- Education institutions (K-12/higher education),
- Research and commercialization resources (universities/corporations/tech transfer),
- Customers (marquee/corporate/consumers),
- Philanthropy (community wealth),
- Government (local, state, and federal), and
- Professional services (legal/accounting/business development).

These assets work together to create new enterprises, jobs, wealth, and economic prosperity. However, unlike natural ecosystems that are organically created, innovation and entrepreneurship ecosystems must be intentionally created.

Law of Economic Competitiveness

No nation can sustainably improve global economic competitiveness without growing exponentially more higher impact employees and higher growth entrepreneurs. If your nation's economic competitiveness goals consistently outpace the growth rate of these people, then your country simply will not—indeed cannot—sustainably increase global economic competitiveness.

Inspired by Packard's Law of Hewlett & Packard Co-Founder, David Packard

Law of Inclusive Competitiveness

No nation can sustainably improve global economic competitiveness without growing exponentially more higher impact employees and higher growth entrepreneurs—which requires the inclusion of disconnected citizens—who create and take advantage of these improved economic conditions.

Inspired by Packard's Law of Hewlett & Packard Co-Founder, David Packard

Non-Equity Citizens

Informed by the equity partner concept in business, non-equity citizens are full and equal citizens under law by birthright or acquisition through naturalization or other legal means. Non-equity citizens are entitled, but not able, to access an equitable proportion of their country's best opportunities and do not hold meaningful underlying economic ownership, wealth, or other interests in their nation. The term is used to distinguish from equity citizens (above).

ScaleUp Partners

ScaleUp is the leading national consultancy advancing *Inclusive Competitiveness* by creating a new, twenty-first century economic narrative and building community systems that improve productivity in the Innovation Economy. By fostering policy, STEAM education, higher growth entrepreneurship, higher impact employment, and risk capital formation and investment, ScaleUp helps improve economic performance by infusing inclusiveness into innovation and entrepreneurship ecosystems, existing and emerging industry clusters, and other sectors critical to increasing economic competitiveness.

T.A.P.I.M. Progression

Inclusive Competitiveness follows the T.A.P.I.M. Progression (Thought, Advocacy, Policy, Investment, Market), which was employed to create existing innovation and entrepreneurship ecosystems and clusters:

- New Thought informs new advocacy,
- New Advocacy produces new policy,
- New Policy *breakthroughs* enable and attract new investments,
- New Investments incent new market behaviors, and
- New Market behaviors deliver new outcomes.

Tipping Point

As defined by Malcolm Gladwell, author of *The Tipping Point: How Little Things Can Make a Big Difference*, a tipping point threshold is the moment that self-sustaining critical mass is achieved. In the context of *Inclusive Competitiveness*, it describes communities on an accelerated downward trajectory that require massive intervention to halt and reverse the decline. The term is used in combination with transformation point and turning point (below).

Transformation Point

Transformation point theory suggests that in order for the transformation process to be triggered within a community, a certain degree of fiscal investment as well as *other types* (i.e., the *IC Framework*) of interventions must be introduced. The term is used in combination with tipping point (above) and turning point (below).

Trim Tab Movement

A series of high-leverage, organized actions and events of national or global scale, yet local in implementation and impact, that take place over an extended period of time and work to achieve exponential impact rather than incremental outcomes.

Trim Tab Organizations

Entities with an operational approach to mission impact based on aggregating key resources, organizing those resources into actionable, collaborative forms, and highly leveraging them to achieve exponential impact rather than incremental outcomes.

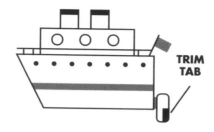

Trim Tabbers

Persons whose capabilities provide the higher leverage leadership needed to turn a matter of importance in the desired direction. Their actions significantly increase the achievement potential of the group, considerably enhancing the probability of mission success and achieving exponential impact rather than incremental outcomes.

Turning Point

As defined by Henry Louis Taylor, Jr. and Sam Cole, University at Buffalo, turning point theory indicates that fiscal investments in a community must rise above a particular threshold before the change process is triggered. The term is used in combination with tipping point (above) and transformation point (above).